ONE FACE

Praise for

ONE FACE

At a certain point in the development of a meaningful career, it is helpful to set aside everything but absolute and unvarnished truth as one considers how the world works. In a disarming and completely authentic way, Sarah McDugal walks through this charming book at your side, with nothing but your best interests at heart. She is your friend, your confidant and your dependable adviser.

—**Andrew Benton**, President & CEO, Pepperdine University

In *One Face*, Sarah elaborates with several wonderful examples the importance of being truthful to one's own conscience; and how that understanding in turn helps in building and improving one's personal and professional relationships.

—**Narayana Murthy**, Founder, InfoSys Limited,
2013 World Entrepreneur of the Year

Sarah McDugal brings nurture to the leadership conversation. *One Face* is motivating, encouraging, concise, clear, effective and efficient. She could have used statistics and facts—and she would have been erudite, eloquent, and excellent—but she chose the less-traveled path of stories, and I thank her for doing so. I will be reading this book over and over again, applying more from *One Face* than any other leadership book I've read.

—**Jason O'Rourke**, Hospital Chaplain, US Army Special Ops

If you are looking for deeper meaning in your work, or you wish to be a more authentic person—*One Face* is your roadmap. I was taught to put your "best foot forward", but that is a slippery slope if you don't know what you stand for. *One Face* explains this problem—and provides unique solutions that are easy to understand and put in place. I understand more after reading this book these rough parts are just another gift in the journey of building values and integrity. I'm glad I was one of the lucky ones to read the book early, as it preserves all the raw enthusiasm and passion that Sarah is known for."

—**Koby Bryan**, CEO Innovative Front, Author of #Integrity

ONE FACE

SHED THE MASK,
OWN YOUR VALUES,
AND LEAD WISELY

SARAH McDUGAL

New York

ONE FACE

SHED THE MASK, OWN YOUR VALUES, AND LEAD WISELY

© 2016 SARAH McDUGAL.

Published in New York, New York, by Morgan James Publishing. Morgan James and The Entrepreneurial Publisher are trademarks of Morgan James, LLC. www.MorganJamesPublishing.com

The Morgan James Speakers Group can bring authors to your live event. For more information or to book an event visit The Morgan James Speakers Group at www.TheMorganJamesSpeakersGroup.com.

Shelfie

A **free** eBook edition is available with the purchase of this print book.

CLEARLY PRINT YOUR NAME ABOVE IN UPPER CASE

Instructions to claim your free eBook edition:
1. Download the Shelfie app for Android or iOS
2. Write your name in **UPPER CASE** above
3. Use the Shelfie app to submit a photo
4. Download your eBook to any device

ISBN 978-1-63047-732-5 paperback
ISBN 978-1-63047-733-2 eBook
Library of Congress Control Number:
2015913008

Cover Design by:
Rachel Lopez
www.r2cdesign.com

Interior Design by:
Bonnie Bushman
The Whole Caboodle Graphic Design

In an effort to support local communities and raise awareness and funds, Morgan James Publishing donates a percentage of all book sales for the life of each book to Habitat for Humanity Peninsula and Greater Williamsburg

Get involved today, visit
www.MorganJamesBuilds.com

Habitat for Humanity®
Peninsula and
Greater Williamsburg
Building Partner

To
All the battered knights on the battlefield.
Because shining armor is totally for rookies.

TABLE OF CONTENTS

FOREWORD

One Face is an inquiry into the values and ethics driving our businesses and our personal lives, and a challenge to insure consistency between the two. Through personal reflections and interviews with business leaders around the globe, the case for establishing a values-driven corporate culture is made – businesses are more reliable and consistent, brands are uncompromised, and the stress of having inconsistent values is alleviated.

Each reader of this book must ask themselves the question: Am I going to live my life and run my business with a fractured moral compass, constantly adjusting my values to meet the situation – or am I going to adhere to my underlying value system and live, work and play authentically?

The author correctly observes: *In personal life, in public leadership and in corporate identity and brand experience it is absolutely vital to choose a set of core values, clearly articulate them and then consistently and intentionally implement them across all platforms.*

I encourage those who read this book to reflect internally and externally to determine if there are any inconsistencies in their value statements and then to correct them. A lifetime of building a good reputation can be ruined by one small lapse of judgment – let your values be your guide.

Rhea Law

Chair, Florida Offices

Buchanan Ingersoll & Rooney

PREFACE

Business leaders fail to achieve long-term success when they don't apply the same set of values internally as they project to their external audience.

This book is for you if…

- you long for less stress and more freedom to be yourself
- you want to make a lasting impact in addition to your profits
- you wish you could know for sure that you're making the right decision every time.

This book is probably NOT for you if…

- you want to cling to the stress of living multiple faces to the world

- you enjoy inspiring contempt among your teammates or employees
- you primarily just want to make money.

In *One Face*, you will learn how to…

- discover and articulate your values
- make decisions focused on longevity
- embrace the gift of feedback and transform it into growth.

At the end of *One Face*, you will possess a clearly defined set of core values, a four-step framework for wise decision-making, and the tools you need to build your brand to last a lifetime.

ACKNOWLEDGMENTS

First, I must thank my parents, Tom and Kathy Matthews, who raised me to value a razor sharp (some would say hyperactive) sense of the difference between right and wrong and a pathological commitment to loyalty. For more than 45 years, they've weathered some of life's perfect storms together and showed me what it means to live with one face.

Second, I owe a tremendous debt of gratitude to my girls: Holly Aamot, Ramona Catarama, Amy Jacobs, Rachel Petersen, and Heather Shurtliff. You have been my sounding boards, my fellow wordsmiths, my comrades in the trenches, my accountability, my bosom friends. And to Kyla Steinkraus, who unofficially edited my entire manuscript before it ever went to the editor. Dearer and truer kindred spirits could not be found.

Third, I'm grateful to the mentors who've lived phenomenal examples of values-driven leadership: Nicole Parker, Walter and June Burn. My undying thanks also goes to those who have modeled unmistakably arrogant and self-centered examples of how *not* to lead. You (hopefully?!) know who you are.

Fourth, I cannot diminish the gifted and generous people who inspired and helped me bring this manuscript to life. Without these rockstars, entire key parts wouldn't exist. Huge thanks goes to Topher Morrison, David Hancock, and Jim Gash. And to Kristen Foht, my editor, who gave invaluable feedback and technical support.

Thank you!

INTRODUCTION

Odds are, you're at one of a few junctures in your experience:

One, you're just starting out. You have a fresh slate, and you are in the process of deciding what foundation your career or business or organization is going to be built upon. You get to pick, you hope you'll choose wisely, and you're praying you'll have the guts to stick with it.

Two, you picked up this book because you've screwed up. You find yourself longing for a refill on your integrity. You recognize the importance of being governed by a single set of core values, yet when you look in the mirror, you see a cracked image, with a dozen fractured faces staring back at you. Unlike some of your colleagues who may be too narcissistic to care, you want that innocence back. You want to shed the stress of being everyone to everyone and find out who you really are.

Three, you've been living with one face already, and you want to help others do so too. You want your brand to stay consistent and trustworthy. You know the profound value and freedom that comes from a commitment to *live with one face.*

LIVE WITH ONE FACE

What does it mean to *live with one face?* It means that integrity comes first. It means that you do what you say you're doing, and that you are who you present yourself to be, both personally and corporately. Living with one face is the ultimate way to shed stress, because you reject the weight of juggling different identities for different environments.

This book isn't a magic pill to unify your segmented existence. But it does have some pretty magical potential if you're willing to get vulnerable. I know, because it reflects my own journey and the journeys of a dozen other people who've shared their stories.

By the time you're done reading, I hope you will have taken the time to articulate the values that drive you, figure out which values don't make the cut, and practice an entirely new framework for making the wisest choice in any given circumstance.

It's my hope that by the time you put this book down, we will have journeyed together into a whole new understanding of authenticity and the freedom it brings.

When you're done reading, I hope you'll be able to go look in the mirror and see only one person looking back at you. And that you'll like and respect who that person is.

When you get there, tweet me a mirror selfie @SarahMcDugal to tell the world you're joining me in the commitment to #live1face.

CHAPTER 1

THE DIGITAL FLIP

> *Souls live at the intersection between our wills, hearts and physical selves. When one is out of harmony with the others, we disintegrate.*
>
> **—Jane E. Stevenson**

It's 3 o'clock in the morning, and I've been at work since 7:00 a.m. yesterday. For the past 20 hours, I've been hyper-focused on running my team's annual general meetings. Our remotely operated international staff has gathered together in Western Europe from more than five different countries to spend a week planning out the next year's projects.

My weary crew members are dropping laptops into backpacks with eyes glazed. We aren't even halfway through the week, and everyone is ready to collapse. We all desperately need sleep, some time off, and a chance to wander cobblestone streets and find inspiration again. I'm about to follow my guys out the door when the boss beckons me into his office.

"Sit down and go over these script concepts with me. I want to add some new projects to the production calendar." He means the calendar we already finished. The one that got voted yesterday, before he tweaked the minutes from the meeting since he didn't like the vote.

I'm exhausted. I'm in a country five time zones away from home and haven't gotten past the jet lag yet. I'm starving because we worked straight through dinner. It takes every remaining ounce of energy to focus my brain out of the fog creeping up on the edges of my vision. At this point, it's all I can do to respond in full sentences.

Oh yes. And yesterday at 5:00 a.m., two little blue lines announced that I'm pregnant. I haven't even told my husband yet. I feel nauseated, but I'm not sure if it's from pregnancy or sheer exhaustion.

Oblivious, my boss isn't even talking about his latest plans to triple the production schedule. I already know it doesn't matter to him that the project lineup was voted. He'll mix it around however he likes, without regard for logic or productivity. He drones on about imaginary insubordination he thinks he has sensed from one or two of our team members. Every couple of days he's convinced that a different person is out to get him. Or to get me. Or somebody else.

I. Could. Not. Care. Less.

My first thought is to protect the current target of his interpersonal paranoia: Why are you slandering the team member who is likely the smartest creative person on our crew (and one of my best friends)? Why are you saying she's after my job? Is it because she and I both stood up to you when you rewrote the voted committee minutes yesterday before sending them out to the team? Is this just malicious payback? His rambling shifts to how he thinks some of the young female team members should take wardrobe lessons from his fashionable and sexy daughter. Then his monologue drifts to daydreaming about exotic vacation plans he's making with his wife.

My next thought is pure self-preservation. Is there any sane reason that this can't wait a mere four hours until 7:00 a.m. when I'm expected to be back at my desk? All I want to do is sleep.

My boss is a narcissistic manipulator, and I'm gradually realizing that I've been enabling him for years. Despite the fact that I'd probably describe myself as someone who reads people well, I'm really only starting to see it for what it is. I've been so busy pandering to his ego, managing his paranoia, and offering myself as a buffer to protect my team from his toxicity that I can't even pinpoint where things went off track.

He's the epitome of a man living different personas to different people. When he's speaking to large crowds around the world, he pontificates ivory tower theories on how to engage in meaningful relationships with people. Off the stage, he rules his support team with an iron dictatorship, keeping us constantly off balance and groveling to please his unpredictable whims. He does not live with one face. He cannot be trusted to do what is right nor to keep his own word, and the entire team knows it. I've stayed this many years because I believe passionately in the work we do, because the reality has crept upon me, because thought I could somehow make it better.

And I don't have a clue how I let things spiral so out of control.

THE WAY THINGS WERE

There was a time when society was made up almost solely of small, intimate social groups. People lived on farms, in villages, in small towns. Even in the big cities, distinct social classes forced narrow circles of interaction. Everybody knew everybody else's story because they grew up alongside each other and then grew old in the same place. If you beat your wife or lied compulsively or cheated customers at your market stall, people knew. They might ignore it, but they still knew. People kept each other's secrets as a matter of survival.

There was a great deal of openness and transparency in this social face-to-face world, but, in contrast, the corporate business world of the industrial age offered consumers little opportunity for fact-checking. The only information you had was the data the company put on paper for you to see. Corporations could essentially tell any story they wanted because it was almost impossible for anyone to uncover the skeletons in their closets, the multiple identities behind closed doors, or their schizophrenic values. This created a very real, opaque corporate veil.

If an organization had a schizophrenic past or a fraudulent present, all you had to do was bury the paper trail, and there was a good chance nobody would ever find the evidence. Even information technically considered "in the public domain" required a time-consuming trip to the county courthouse or an archives building. Then you had to sit in a file room and sneeze your way through a hundred mildewy boxes until you found that one elusive sheet of paper. You had to possess an intense investigative drive—or a search warrant—to ever hope to unveil corporate secrets.

Those large corporations also controlled the media, which meant they controlled the story. A select few at the top determined the message, the morals, and the mindset they wished to instill among the public. The corporate veil protected big companies and shielded the shenanigans of their leadership from public view. It was fairly easy to hide the skeletons in your corporate closet in the analog world.

That was then.

THE DIGITAL FLIP

Now we have the reverse.

You might naturally think this means that the opaque veil has been pulled back, since so much information is out in the open. But instead of vanishing, the veil has simply repositioned itself. Now, rather than keeping corporate secrets hidden away, we've allowed it to separate us individually through a constant façade of digital media.

In real life, we now tend to exist in isolated, compartmentalized worlds where we rarely speak to neighbors, and where anybody can pose as anybody else on the Internet. The digital world gives every person with a WiFi connection the platform to pretend to be anyone they wish, for any purpose, a luxury once available only to wealthy businesses. Identity reinvention awaits, available at the stroke of our fingertips. Any teenage kid in a chat room knows it's challenging to resist the lure of presenting ourselves as someone we're not, simply because digital media makes it so easy for us to do so. And those on the other side of the screen have no way of knowing if you're the 13-year-old girl you say you are or a dangerous criminal. There's no way to know the difference.

If you're a jerk, or a narcissist, or a fraud, or a pedophile, the digital veil can allow you to successfully conceal your true self for a very long time. Interestingly, since the veil has flipped, it also allows the average person to more successfully navigate around what was once such an opaque corporate protection. Three dozen keystrokes on Google can reveal anything that is a matter of public record anywhere, and can often expose a significant amount of so-called private data as well. Corporate skeletons are no longer so easily closeted away.

We're living in the center of this digital flip. Unless we make a focused, intentional effort to seek transparency, while simultaneously rejecting the temptation to compare our behind-the-scenes with everyone else's social media highlight reel, we don't stand a chance at authenticity.

Whether you are a corporate leader, a brand manager, a non-profit visionary, or simply a caring individual, you're telling a story with your life and through your organization. All relationships are based on trust. That trust is either strengthened or destroyed by the values people observe you acting out on a day-to-day basis. When there is a breakdown between what happens in a leader's private life and the message they present to their public, or between a company's published philosophy and the experience someone has with an employee or product—trust is broken.

Nothing kills brand engagement and violates trust faster than feeling betrayed, believing you'd bought into a relationship that offered one particular set of values, and then discovering that the reality is something different. Examples such as Enron and Bill Cosby come to mind.

In personal life, in public leadership, and in corporate identity and brand experience, it is absolutely vital to choose a set of core values, clearly articulate them, and then consistently and intentionally implement them across all platforms.

If all facets of your individual leadership or your organization are not governed by the same set of values, you will end up dividing your effectiveness by spending at least some of your energy putting a positive spin on the skeletons in your closet and investing the rest of that energy into making sure no one opens the closet door.

The looming challenge we all face in both corporate and individual identity is our deep and rooted human need to *live with one face*.

CHAPTER 2

I NEVER MEANT TO END UP HERE

It takes 20 years to build a reputation and 5 minutes to ruin it. If you think about that, you'll do things differently.
—Warren Buffett

The years I spent working for that particularly narcissistic manipulator were some of the best of my life. It sounds counter-intuitive, but I'm grateful for the experience. That job allowed me to travel the world, producing events and directing media projects I'd never imagined possible. I was privileged to work with amazing team members—outstanding, talented, passionate individuals who were also conscientious professionals.

For a 20-something fresh out of graduate school, I was given a remarkable amount of freedom, at first. Freedom to be creative, to hone my skills, to manage a creative team, to partner with people who inspired positive and tangible change within our target demographic. I got to explore my natural leadership strengths and taste the satisfaction of making massive social impact by creating resources for international community development agencies, producing short films for global broadcast that taught positive messages for families, and mentoring younger media professionals into fulfilling careers.

It was a dream job. The satisfaction was there; the fulfillment was there. I had constant opportunities to indulge my wanderlust, traveling to exotic places like Australia, Russia, the Netherlands—directing video productions, developing training resources, speaking to crowds of hundreds and sometimes thousands. Everything was amazing—except for the situation with my boss.

So why did I put up with him for so long?

I truly believed in the work our team was doing. That was one of the good reasons. One of the not-so-great reasons was that I was far too trusting. Of course, it wasn't so bad at first. You rarely leap directly into a toxic relationship or an abusive environment. Rather, it creeps upon you by degrees. All the little opportunities where you silenced the warning in your gut and went along with something that didn't quite feel right—those add up over time. Little choices that seemed neutral but weren't—yet you couldn't see reality for what it was until you got enough puzzle pieces in place.

THE COST OF MISPLACED TRUST

I was too young, trusting, and completely under his charismatic spell, in the beginning, to realize that this work I loved so much was permanently throttled by the reality that the top leader did not live with transparent authenticity behind closed doors. After all, I was in my late 20s and already the associate director of an international non-profit. Wasn't that worth putting up with some frustrations? So what if I have a pesky boss. Doesn't everyone?

For a long time, I dismissed his power-hungry behavior as merely the reality of having a grown-up job in a grown-up world, where the top brass are naturally expected to be capricious, demanding, paranoid, and petty. I spent years excusing and enabling him, buffering the abuse from my team, until that exhausted encounter in the wee hours when it dawned on me just how precarious everything had become.

Not long after, my crew was ready to quit, the overseeing board began investigating my boss on multiple allegations of sexual harassment, and the entire organization was in danger of crumbling because the guy at the top didn't live with one face. Because his public and private personas were not governed by an aligned set of core values.

For years, I told myself that as long as I lived with integrity, I could protect the team and our audience from the toxic internal state of affairs. I took it upon myself to try to be the glue for all these fractures. But I was both asking too much of myself, and giving myself too much credit at the same time. Looking back, I should have confronted it head-on in a values-driven, integrity-driven way instead of just hoping it would get better and praying I could manage the fallout.

When a corporate culture is fractured behind the scenes—unless those fractures are addressed and repaired—no project, no company, no cause, no individual leader will reach their full potential. And no one single person can be expected to bridge the gaps in someone else's integrity. Every single person, including the boss, must be held responsible to maintain their own personal integrity.

Fortunately, even the most unscrupulous boss can teach life-changing lessons. One of the greatest lessons I learned from that experience was how *not* to manage my teams. Thanks to him, I now operate under a completely opposite philosophy of team management.

If it was great—my team did it.
If it was okay—we did it.
If it was a complete bust—I did it.

It doesn't matter who on the team was responsible; we'll sort out responsibility and ways to improve within the team, in private. Any leadership decision I make, as long as it's the opposite of what that former boss would have done, I'll probably be in the clear. I do not expect perfection, but I do demand transparency.

From a team management viewpoint, those brutal years taught me the value of building infrastructure differently by focusing on:

- clear communication,
- timely conflict resolution,

- transparent goals,
- complete loyalty, and
- absolutely no skeletons stashed in the closet.

From a client management viewpoint, those years taught me not only to act with integrity but also to never over-trust. It's wise to listen when your instincts say "there's a red flag here" instead of sitting back and hoping it won't get too bad, or assuming you can manage the fallout. Now, if I discover that a client has unaddressed skeletons in the closet or is living with a fractured set of conflicting values, I simply decline to work with them. I won't present their product. I won't promote them.

Unless, of course, they're tired of living a double life, and they have come to me for a complete reboot.

You're sitting there asking, "But doesn't that result in a loss of work?"

Yep. Absolutely.

And I'm okay with that. Because the same clients who have a low threshold on honesty are going to be the ones who run my team ragged and then argue over the bill. Rather than slipping from one crisis management to the next, this philosophy means we are free to create outstanding quality projects for clients who actually appreciate it.

I'd rather spend my time helping good clients become great, than massaging the egos of hopelessly narcissistic ones. Really, you could probably just call it naked self-preservation.

WHAT? NO PRIVATE LIFE?

This *does not* mean you don't get to have both a public and a private life. When you are on a public platform as an individual leader or your organization is communicating with your audience, you naturally have public and private realities. Totally not the same thing as public face and private face.

This means you are not governed by different sets of public and private values. If you catch yourself thinking "Which of my values are acceptable among this group?" then you're already in trouble. If you have to ask yourself that question, you're likely well into the process of adding skeletons to your closet. You're not *living with one face*.

Living with one face means you don't have to invest energy into covering up aspects of your life or putting a positive spin on the skeletons someone discovered—because you simply don't have any skeletons to hide.

Living with one face means you don't try to advertise your awesome non-GMO "good for you" product while hoping no one spills the secret that your factories are powered by slave labor in China. If your company chooses to outsource to questionable suppliers, you don't have the freedom to get bent out of shape when someone calls you to task for it.

Ever checked an iPhone to see where it's made? Apple makes only one claim: "designed in the USA." Anyone who reads the news knows Apple's products are assembled in the cheapest possible environment in places like China. To be fair, Apple's brand isn't about sustainability or fair trade in the least. They don't even pretend to hide where their products are assembled. Their brand is about innovation and design and intuitively user-friendly products. If they were making claims of being environmentally green or manufacturing through fair trade, then Apple would be living a lie. But they're not wasting money trying to convince people of a value the company doesn't hold in the first place. Instead, they publicly own their ethically questionable reality as the avenue by which they are able provide the Western world with innovative technical luxury. So, ultimately, their external message is in line with their corporate brand values. (Whether or not that leaves you still feeling okay with buying Apple products is up to you.)

When you live with multiple faces, there's an incredible amount of stress required just to maintain a façade of normalcy. You have to keep track of what you said when and where and to whom, and which people you can do which things around. Energy that could be expended on creative productivity is lost in the black hole of juggling identities.

This doesn't merely affect you personally. Imagine the tension and stress in the life of a woman who knows (or strongly suspects) she is married to a pedophile, but she puts on a happy normal face every weekend in church. Or the man who has a beautiful and engaging wife who is the belle of every dinner party, until the company leaves, and her nagging and yelling begins. Or the corporate division that claims to sell all-natural products but keeps the ingredient list a trade secret precisely because it includes carcinogenic formaldehyde derivatives.

In essence, every company must discern which values are most inherent to their identity and then be brave enough to live them out. Apple brands itself on the values of innovation and style, and is unapologetic about the fact that it does not value fair trade sourcing. They go for luxury, and they don't compete on price.

When you know who you are, you can operate with confidence. You can charge a higher price. And you don't waste time with media spin for skeletons in your closet because you either have none or you simply own them and move on. When your company lives with one face, people trust you to make good on your expected behaviors, whatever those may be.

Every grossly exaggerated breakdown of core values originally began with a few small choices. Choices nobody thought really mattered.

You know how you feel let down when your favorite celebrity turns out to be a total scumbag? Bill Cosby makes a perfect example. He built a lifetime platform based on clean comedy, family values, and telling young men around the world to stand up and respect their wives and provide for their families. But behind the scenes, he was allegedly drugging and raping dozens of vulnerable women.

That sense of betrayal runs deep. It makes you question whether his great public message was ever actually honest. How could someone who believed his own statements about values and ethics be guilty of abusing women in private? Suddenly, nothing he says holds the same weight. Instead of being an authority on how to build strong family with a sense of humor, he's now viewed by many as just another powerful abuser.

WHAT'S MY STORY GOT TO DO WITH IT?

As a child, I grew up in a screen-free home. We had no television, watched no videos, owned no computer, and never, ever went to the theater. Instead, we read books. Not the twaddle so easily found on children's bookshelves today. We read real books. Books about well-known leaders and also about people I'd never hear about in school. Biographies. Auto-biographies. Allegories. Rare vintage tales. History. Literature.

For my sixth birthday, my parents gifted me with a paperback copy of John Bunyan's Pilgrim's Progress, in the original English. I devoured it cover to cover. Yes, I know. Total #nerdintraining.

I would read for hours at a time. Tales of heroes, explorers, inventors, scientists, spies, missionaries—all fascinated me. I fell captivated under the spell of ordinary people who displayed extraordinary grit—everyday heroes whose lives were so closely aligned to their core values that they refused to allow the most daunting outside circumstances to dictate them as failures.

Stories about people like:

- David Livingstone, who taught himself ancient languages at the age of 8, while working long hours in Great Britain's child-powered weaving factories.
- Booker T. Washington, who was born into Virginian slavery, worked in the mines even after emancipation, and then became a powerful political and social leader.

- Susannah Wesley, who birthed 19 children, raised 10 of them to adulthood including the famous John & Charles, and taught each one how to read on the day they turned 5. She wrote in her diary that one daughter was a bit mentally slow, because she took a day and a half to learn her alphabet, but forgave her when by age 8 she could fluently read New Testament Greek.
- Corrie ten Boom's bravery during World War II while enduring Ravensbruck for hiding Jews in her home.
- Brother Andrew's hair-raising accounts of God making "seeing eyes blind" while he transported faith-based literature hidden in plain sight on trips behind the Iron Curtain.
- Waldemar Jesske's boyhood survival when his family was banished to Siberia because of their ancestral ethnicity.
- John G. Paton's terrifying Thirty Years with South Sea Cannibals, living on a dangerous island and forgotten by Western civilization.
- Serpouhi Tavoukdjian's traumatic teenage genocide survival during the 1915 Armenian Death March, rescued from imminent death only by being sold by her mother into slavery.

If the tales you absorb during childhood shape your aspirations, then I dreamt of triumph over tragedy, harrowing humanitarian adventures, and ultimately changing the world.

I didn't realize it then, but the common thread weaving between all of these people was the value system embedded in each hero's character. These were not people who would call themselves heroes. Their very nature would rebel at such a flamboyant label. But they never deviated from the values that drove them, or when they did, they set an example of how to learn from one's mistakes and come back stronger. Their values were everything that mattered.

Stories stick. They emote.

As powerful as stories are, I really can't comprehend why so much of today's world insists on structuring education and proving leadership based on facts and statistics. It's as though we've convinced ourselves stories are best left for children, and grownups don't need that crutch in order to make wise, motivated decisions. Of course, I believe facts need to be accurate, and statistics can drive home a great point. But they rarely move people to action the way a gripping story can. They don't inspire lasting change. Dry facts are generally quite forgettable.

Stories? Experiences? Not so much.

A multi-sensory experience, whether it is with a brand or a person or a great book, becomes part of your own story. It carves out a space inside your being and alters the way you process reality. You're never really the same again. The effects linger and continue to transform over time.

And that's exactly why every leader, every brand, and every organization needs to embrace and harness the power of their own unique values. Because the values are the engine that drives the storyline. Those values *must be* consistent with their overall identity. Throughout the rest of this book, I'm going to share stories from companies who have succeeded in doing just that.

CONVERSATIONS | EVERETT BOWES | VISUAL CREATIVES, INC.

I met Everett Bowes on LinkedIn. Meaning, he sent me a connection request, I accepted, and the resulting exchange of messages was interesting enough that we scheduled a phone call. Everett is a leader in brand strategy and organizational culture. He used to introduce himself as a professional in BrandStory, but since every fifth person on the planet started calling themselves a "storyteller," he feels that title has gotten a tad watered down. Now he's looking for a new way to describe his work that hasn't been hijacked by fakers. Meantime, he shared some incredible insights on how companies keep missing the mark in building a strong, compelling and cohesive brand.

Sarah: So often I meet people who realize that their company could be doing better, and when I say that they need a stronger brand, they reply "But I've got a logo. I've got letterhead. I have a sign on my front door. What's your point?" They don't realize that those are some of the smallest components of a brand. They fail to see that their inconsistent values and fractured consumer experience are driving people away. Your brand is so much more than just a logo! It is the sum of your friends, values, behaviors, and the habits people grow to expect of you.

Everett: Exactly. The knee-jerk reaction is, "We've already done all that. We have a website, a color palette, a style guide." Other times, I'm called in to lead a brand discovery session, and they say "We've already done that, too. We have a mission statement on our brochure." But I guarantee they've not done it thoroughly because a quick look at their brand experience reveals a massive misalignment in their identity.

Sarah: How would you define identity misalignment?

Everett: To me, the essence of a brand is its expected behavior. Imagine two people standing side by side. On the left is a biker named Spike; he's wearing all black, has a long beard, aviator sunglasses, leather vest, and is leaning on his Harley Davidson. To the right is Elle from the movie "Legally Blonde." When you look at these two people, it's easy to see that their identity dictates a lot of their expected behavior. Is there a contrast in expectations based on their appearance? Based on their names? Of course. You're not going to expect the same identifying behaviors from two people called Spike and Elle.

What language do you expect to hear out of Spike? What language do you assume will come from Elle? What about style and colors? If it's black and rugged, he'll wear it. If it's pink and frilly, she'll wear it.

Imagine their homes, their furniture. She's going to have designer items and high-end art; he's likely to have milk crates and a couch from Goodwill. Of course there's always someone out there who doesn't fall into the stereotypes, but in general your personal identity dictates everything from nickname to vocabulary, to tone of voice, to level of health, to favorite colors, clothing choices, household furnishings, attitudes under pressure, values, and integrity. That unique combination that makes you *you*, is also what ultimately dictates your behavioral habits. If you accidentally step on their foot in a crowded restaurant, Spike and Elle will likely react very differently. The same reality applies to brands.

When a company says "Oh, we've already had a brand identity exercise—we know who we are," you can see this misalignment. You may be pricing yourself as designer luxury. But in practice, you're the equivalent of milk crates and junkyard furniture.

Look at your office. How does your workspace align with the brand values you're trying to position on social media? What I call "brand identity multiple personality disorder" is this misalignment from conflicting brand experiences.

Sarah: This is the kind of assessment and consultation I do on a regular basis, whether it's for heavyweight businesses or aspiring musicians who want to improve their consistency.

Everett: Some companies will say "Oh you're creating a persona." No, I'm not. A persona tends to be information driven. It's going to touch your head. Solid brand development goes much deeper than that. I am trying to find that emotional connection that will touch your heart. All brand experiences must resonate with the driving values that make up the brand identity. It impacts everything—in the same way Elle would never wear Adidas sneakers and Spike doesn't even know who Jimmy Choo is.

Sarah: So how would you describe brand value?

Everett: Look at Apple. I actually worked there years ago. Apple is one of the most valuable brands in the world. I'm not talking about trust; I'm talking about revenue. Does their brand identity impact their décor?

Sarah: Absolutely. So much so that other brands around the world now describe a certain look as "Apple-inspired."

Everett: Does their brand identity impact their values? Does it impact their integrity? Steve Jobs' father was a furniture guy who built kitchen cabinets. He always painted the back of the cabinets, the part that gets nailed to the wall. Somebody asked him "Why are you painting the back side of the cabinet? No one's going to see it!" He said, "Yeah, but I know it's there." That trickled down to Steve, when he created the first Mac computers. Each engineer signed the inside of the cases they made. Long before people opened computers to change hard drives, Steve Jobs saw Apple products as art that was worthy of signatures on the inside.

Sarah: So you're saying that brand identity, the organizational personality, impacts every decision. A successful brand allows the company's personality to extend consistently into every aspect of user experience.

Everett: Businesses fail when they lose predictability. If you have a problem with a product you bought from Nordstrom, do you have any doubt how they're going to handle it when you take that product back to them?

Sarah: Nope. Not a bit.

Everett: No doubt whatsoever. What about if you have a problem with your order at McDonalds?

Sarah: No, they stand behind their product.

Everett: With well-branded businesses, you have the ability to make expectations and predictions about their behavior based on the values they have set for themselves. Why did people line up in droves to buy the very first iPhone? It wasn't even in their hands yet. Because there is only one Apple. We know that the past products were amazing, and we've emotionally bought into the brand. Before ever holding an iPhone, people knew that Apple believes in great design, great technology, and a simple interface that will make your life better.

However, the day Apple loses that oneness with their values, their brand will completely split. If they ever sell a lower quality version and at the regular price, then suddenly you have no idea what Apple brand you're dealing with. The trust and integrity is gone.

Sarah: It's a trust factor tied in with a heavily integrated user experience that reinforces the same values down to the smallest details. In order to be a leader—whether that means being a celebrity or a corporate leader or making your company an industry leader—you must have a single set of core values driving your internal and external face.

Everett: You cannot have multiple sets of values for inside and outside that fluctuate depending on environment. What people see must be what they get. And if it's not, then you have to be committed to making it right.

CHAPTER 3

LIVING LEJIT

When your values are clear to you, making decisions becomes easier.

—Roy E. Disney

I probably couldn't count the number of times I've been let down by a leader I'd respected. You meet someone, read their book, hear them speak, and no matter how adult you are, you catch yourself thinking, "Wow, that person is amazing. I wanna be just like them when I grow up!"

Then, some indefinite time period later, you learn they cheated on their spouse or embezzled money or plagiarized "their" content, and you feel utterly deflated. Guess I don't wanna be them after all… Bummer.

Sometimes it's closer to home—a boss, mentor, or significant other whom you admired or even loved.

When you discover that this person is an utter jerk, or a narcissist, or a fraud in private life, it can shake your faith not only in them personally but also in humanity at large.

As a leader, you are left with essentially two options: 1) keep your public and private faces separate and hope no one unmasks your fractured existence, or 2) you can shed the mask, own your values, and *live with one face*.

I've already said it, but just to clarify, I don't mean leaders shouldn't have private lives. As a business owner, social leader, mentor, and wife of a community leader, I freely acknowledge great value in keeping one's personal life personal. But you can't indefinitely get away with having multiple faces.

I'm talking about being the same core person no matter which environment you're in at the moment—home, work, play, travel. I'm talking about embracing your core values within every facet of your leadership. Not based on who you wish people thought you were, not based on the expectations of whichever social circle you're in at the moment. Private and public interactions must be driven by an identical set of values. Otherwise, one of your faces is living a lie.

Here are seven reasons why it is crucial to live with one face. Because it challenges you to:

1. *be real.* When you aren't in denial of who you really are, then the pressure is on to be a decent person all the time. You've got to live with one face, not several,

which forces you to look in the mirror and decide whether you like the identity that is truly you. (And if you're not satisfied, then it challenges you to find ways to become somebody you actually want to see looking back at you, but I digress.)

2. *be focused.* When you're transparent about what drives you, it's easier to avoid those enticing distractions. Verbally opening up about bits and pieces of your story throughout daily life provides a constant reminder of why you do what you do. It keeps you grounded in the process that got you here.

3. *be honest.* You're no more perfect than I am, which means we're all messed up on some level. Finding the courage to face failures and admit past mistakes gives you a platform to transform them for good. Not only do you get to repeatedly benefit from your own lessons, but sharing your hard-won wisdom also creates authentic connection points for mentoring others. And when you aren't hiding parts of yourself, there's a lot more space to breathe easy.

4. *be kind.* Living with one face naturally comes easier if you are actually a kind person. Kindness, combined with honesty, inspires a greater ability to trust the kindness of others. Being kind shouldn't be a means to an end. Being kind isn't about manipulating others to gain trust for later exploitation. Genuine kindness should be its own end-game—its own point.

5. *be a listener.* It may seem counterintuitive, but your values don't affect only you. Neither do mine. We are

each impacted by the choices of those with whom we interact. And we each affect others as we make our own choices. Depending on your personality, it can be as equally challenging to shut up and listen as it is to open up and share. But when you do, you begin to realize that the sum of each story is far greater than its individual parts, and life is richer for taking the time to listen.

6. *be humble.* Put simply, you cannot last as a respected leader while simultaneously manipulating and using people around you. Narcissistic, self-absorbed leaders deftly compartmentalize life into multiple identities and may be skilled at keeping those faces separate. However, the ultimate result is a sense of abuse, contempt, and betrayal from their team members. Living one single transparent face is a catalyst to rejecting narcissism and embracing humility.

7. *be accountable.* When you view yourself or your company as a small part of a much greater whole, you realize that your goal, career, ministry, or purpose is something far exceeding the reaches of your ego. Anything you create, any team you build needs to be strong and diverse enough to outlast your own tenure. Accountability keeps that potential alive.

DISCOVER YOUR VALUES

It's 2008—it's been five years since our wedding, and this weekend some of our friends keep saying we just have to attend an all-day workshop with them called "Family iD." My husband wants to go. It's supposed to be amazing.

I think it sounds ridiculous. Maybe it would be amazing—if we had kids. But we don't have kids. We aren't even planning to try for kids any time soon. Why should I go and waste my only free day this weekend at a family coaching seminar?

We go anyway.

LEJIT

There were a lot of funny stories about parenting—as you'd expect. What I didn't expect was to discover some of the most powerful leadership and branding concepts I've ever learned anywhere. "Every family is headed somewhere, but few get there on purpose," said Greg Gunn, the dynamic powerhouse-dad behind Family iD's non-profit organization (www.family-id.com). "Do you know your top core values? Have you written them down? Are you passing them intentionally to the next generation?"

I sat in that workshop, stumped by questions I'd have thought I could answer easily. I stared at lists of different values, circled the 30 that jumped out at me, then narrowed to my top 15, and then trimmed again to the five I just couldn't live without. It was grueling.

But it was worth it.

By the end of the day, I had defined with certainty the things in life which mattered most to me and which values transcended the appreciated into the non-negotiable. Those values are:

- L-oyalty
- E-xcellence
- J-ustice
- I-ntegrity
- T-ransparency

I joke that for me, these are the qualities that make any decision LEJIT. No, it's not properly spelled, but using the misspelled version is a way to help me remember not only the list, but also the power of legitimacy they hold over me. These are the qualities I can't live without. In their absence, I become a frustrated, unfulfilled, and unfocused mess.

On the other hand, the pursuit of these five values wakes me up. The projects I love most are those that center around bringing justice, building trust, and developing excellence. Sure, I can do other things, but they don't make me feel alive. Pursuits outside my sphere of values make me feel reduced to just another cog in someone else's machine. Which, I might add, is a feeling I really hate.

This is also why I experienced such a wrenching dichotomy with the toxic work situation in my opening story. The actual work being done in that job was deeply fulfilling my core values, even while the manipulative and untrustworthy behavior of my boss was at odds with those values. It was excruciating to leave the work that I loved in order to candidly confront the fact that the environment was unsustainable.

The Family iD workshop took place perhaps a year before that hungry and exhausted night in Europe when I realized there was no going back from this toxic boss. If I hadn't already articulated my values, I might never have had the courage to stand for what I knew was right, in the face of someone I perceived to be much more powerful than myself.

Knowing my core values ultimately brought me freedom. Freedom to say "Yes!" to amazing opportunities. But also the freedom to know when to say "No." The resulting sense of confidence in who I am and where I want to go with my life, was priceless.

The same is true of leadership teams and organizations. We're all headed someplace. But are you getting there on purpose? Are you getting there with honesty and integrity and a sense of peace—with one face? Or are you focused more on surviving the demands of the day than on intentional decisions toward your desired goal?

One crucial difference between going places and getting there on purpose, lies in the process of answering one simple set of questions:

- What drives your goals?
- What ignites your passion?
- What is so important to you that you'd be willing to die to protect it?
- What wakes you each morning, revved and raring to go?
- What's your metric for determining personal priorities?
- How do you know which opportunities to say "No" to?
- Which values don't matter to you at all?

The answer to every question is discovered most effectively in the process of articulating your core values.

If you're looking in the mirror and you see all of these different identities staring back at you, then it is time to invest some serious thought and self-reflection to decide which person is really YOU.

GO AHEAD, SHED THE STRESS

Without a single overarching set of core values, some day your brand will fold. Or, instead of working harder to cover up the inconsistencies, you could pick an identity and stick with it.

Your individual brand is essentially your reputation. So whether it's a corporate brand that falls apart when someone blows the whistle on the skeletons in the closet or your personal reputation that's shattered when someone finds out you're not who you say you are, unpleasantness is guaranteed. That's something people too often don't take into consideration. We want ourselves and our company to look good, but how often do we ask, "Is this about more than just looking good on the façade? Does it go all the way to the bone?"

The absence of this awareness is one huge reason many businesses are short-lived. And it's also a driving factor in why team leaders fail to garner trust and respect. People sense when a leader is living multiple realities, even if they can't put their finger on it. And there's a huge amount of stress on the leader, because if one or more of your faces is lying, you've got to keep that straight.

If you're saying, "This is me! This is my company!" then you're not alone. But before you jump headlong into applying this values exploration to your corporate brand, focus on yourself. No organization can grow effectively if the leader is not willing to be stretched. Do you like the person who looks back in the mirror? Is that reflection one you want your children to emulate? Or do you need a turnaround?

Once you've determined what you personally stand for, start asking the same questions from scratch for your business. If you know your business isn't performing at its highest potential, very likely a large part of the reason is that nobody has articulated the core values and identity of the organization. No one knows what story to tell. No one knows exactly which face to show. Maybe your leadership does not come across as transparent, maybe you appear distracted, maybe you haven't realized that discovering and articulating your values is a process important enough to be worth significant time and attention. Whatever the reason, that scattered lack of focus will reveal itself in the way experiences are branded and how your organization's identity is presented. Even if the schizophrenia can't be described or clearly quantified, it can be felt. This works against your brand and detracts from the engagement and loyalty of your target market.

It is just as important to articulate the values you don't care about as it is to outline the ones you cherish. You need to declare what your company is willing to stand for and reinforce what is free to be ignored. If you go to a high-end dealer and try to buy a BMW for the price of a Honda, the sales guys are simply not going to have that discussion with you. If you go in saying, "Hey, I'm torn between BMW and Audi because I think Audi might have some features I like better," now they're happy to talk. It doesn't bother them at all to lose your sale based on price—delivering a cheap car is not in their value structure. But if you want to debate luxury features, they're going to do everything they can to gain your business.

The corporate brand representatives (also called salespeople) of any successful luxury car dealer know clearly which values they care about and which ones don't matter to their business. It takes the pressure off even the newest rookie sales guy, because he knows there's no way he's expected to negotiate a sale for a guy who wants a new BMW for a used-Ford price.

There's an incredible amount of tension involved in maintaining multiple faces. It's exhausting to try to be everything to everyone and to constantly be second-guessing what you actually stand for. If that goes on long enough, it will affect every other aspect of life.

FREE GIVEAWAY!

Download my free worksheet guide to discovering and articulating your own core values at www.SarahMcDugal.com/free-stuff/.

CONVERSATIONS | BILL POLK | STORE MANAGER

Bill Polk isn't the hard-driving corporate CEO-type; instead, he's the store manager at our local tire repair place. There's nothing fancy about his shop, except how you're treated when you walk in. People comment about it around town, although they can't quite put their finger on it. "Bill's guys all kind of act the same. They treat you with respect and courtesy, and they make sure the job's done right." I'd heard these glowing rumors and decided to get to know Bill for myself. Naturally, I asked for his perspective on how his guys earned this reputation.

Sarah: I keep running into people in town who think the world of you, not least being my husband and my mom. If you get a quality vote from both of them, you've gotta be onto something.

Bill: [laughs] I don't know if that's good or bad, but I'm glad to see it shows through.

Sarah: Definitely a good thing! So do you train your guys to be this way, or do you only hire people who already fit that mold? How do you create that cohesiveness as a team leader?

Bill: I don't want to sound like a tyrant, but it's my way or the highway. [laughter] You do it my way, or I'll find somebody else who will. On the other hand, I have a very laid-back approach to leadership. I take a lot of input from my guys and consider their thoughts and feelings before I make a rash decision. They know their feedback matters. We work side by side and very closely together and that is the way I build the team.

Sarah: In other words, you have a non-negotiable expectation for excellence, but a deep respect for the interpersonal dynamics among your team. Does that mean you hire for character instead of skills?

Bill: Very much so. When I interview somebody, I don't focus on what you've done. I look for personality. I can teach somebody to do things well, but the integrity has to match. It's paramount to have the quality character, for more than one reason. Number one, for honesty, because I don't want customers worried about things being stolen. Secondly, they've got to mesh with the other guys in the shop. I know my guys, their personalities, weaknesses, and strengths.

Sarah: You don't want somebody uprooting or exploiting that.

Bill: Exactly. My new guy is just now starting to mesh. It's taken a while because he's more intelligent than anybody I've hired before. He's not the grunt mechanic type. He doesn't fit the brash, conceited, hands-on-intelligence-only mold. He's book smart, and that's good, but the other guys are just now starting to bring him in. But he's honest and teachable—that's key.

Sarah: How do you manage to dictate such an exact level of excellence while keeping a positive dynamic among your team?

Bill: It's all training. I know exactly what our company stands for and exactly how things are supposed to be done. I make sure that new guys coming in are thoroughly trained. And if there is a desire to experiment outside of those protocols, I'll go say, "Okay, let's talk about this. The company's way follows logical sequence. It's been tested over the past 40 years for efficiency and excellence and streamlined into the fastest order.

Sarah: So they know you're not being capricious and arbitrary.

Bill: No, it's never just "because I said so." I won't work for somebody like that, and I won't be that kind of boss. Sometimes a new guy just has to do things his way, or he was trained differently, but every single time we show him our system, he'll step back and go, "Wow! That made sense."

Sarah: So your company's values of excellence are backed up by solidly established technical structures that give you a great sense of confidence and pride in what you do.

Bill: Absolutely. Every job is performed the same way every time. Our systems have built-in steps to double check our work, and if my guys follow that system, we'll almost never get customers coming back to complain. I expect nothing less from my team, and they respect me for it.

Sarah: It sounds like a military-level of hierarchy.

Bill: Maybe because I spent 15 years in the military? That's where I get my structure from. That's why I'm comfortable in this type of a learning environment.

Sarah: How do you balance that level of demand with the relationships to keep a team well-oiled?

Bill: There is no "balance." When I hire people, I tell them going in that they are going to do it a specific way. Clear expectations, well-articulated values for both individuals and the company, and a defined outline for how each job is supposed to be done means that everybody knows exactly who we are and how we do things.

Sarah: So let's go back to that respect you mentioned…

Bill: Yes. My guys respect and trust me. And I trust them. I can sit here having this conversation with you in my office without worrying, because my shop is running smoothly back there. The managers before me were having the crew do work under the table, never paying them for their time, stealing from the company. If anything went wrong, those managers threw their team under the bus to corporate. My guys know that if corporate calls me, my answer will be "I made a mistake, I'm sorry," and I'll take the brunt of it for them.

Sarah: In other words, they know you've got their back and that translates into a tight team loyalty. What are the top three or five core values that drive you and your team?

Bill: *Trust*, that's huge. If I can't trust them and they can't trust me, there's no point in being on the same team. *Honesty*, because if they've messed up a car, I want them to come and say, "I made a mistake and I broke this." *Responsibility*. If you've done it wrong, tell me you've done it wrong. I can fix it much quicker if the car is still here than if the customer comes back frustrated. *Accountability*, for the same reasons. I guess that's the gist of it.

Sarah: Now, here's a bit of a personal question. Are those your same core values off the job?

Bill: Absolutely. I'm a father. A husband. A Christian. Without those roles, I'm nobody. And I'm not what I used to be. That's hard to talk about. At one time, I was trapped living a bunch of different identities.

Sarah: How did that change?

Bill: I got tired! I would come to work as one person and go home as another person, and I felt like a chameleon. If a guy came in driving his pickup truck, I'd be good ol' Bill. If a guy came in driving a Cadillac rolling on 24s, I could be down wit' it too, dawg. And when I'd go home, I was completely different again.

Sarah: Worn-out Bill, by that point?

Bill: I was exhausted. And it all collided when I became a Christian. One day, my preacher asked me directly, "Who is Bill Polk?" I said, "Can I get back with you on that? There are so many different versions of me that it's gonna take a while for me to have an answer." He said, "Go home, think about it, and tell me who Bill Polk is."

After a few days, I still had no answer. That's when I realized there is one good person inside me, and I need to bring him wherever I go. Now I'm the same person; I don't care who walks in the door. Now, I'm father and daddy and husband—Bill.

Sarah: How did you decide which one to keep?

Bill: I kept the only guy I liked.

Sarah: The one you wanted to see in the mirror.

Bill: Exactly, the one I was proud of. The genuine Bill Polk. All the other guys were façades. I'm a service manager, the store manager, the counter relations guy; I'm the parts manager, the shop foreman, the dispatcher. I do everything. If I'm doing all that, plus I've got to juggle 10 different personalities, that makes for a long day. As one person, my day is long enough.

Sarah: Thank you for being honest and real and vulnerable. One last question, what do you feel makes your team stand out from your competitors?

Bill: Go back to the core values. Honesty, trust, accountability, responsibility. A lot of my competitors are loss leaders. They'll undermine my price to get you in the door, but by the time you leave, you'll be paying more for the same services. I'm transparent in everything that I do.

Sarah: I'd say *transparency* might be your fifth core value.

Bill: Hey, I'm stupid, and I like it simple. Don't need to complicate things! I just aim to do things the right way, and everything else takes care of itself.

CHAPTER 4

KISSING FROGS

In any moment of decision, the best thing you can do is the right thing. The worst thing you can do is nothing.
—Theodore Roosevelt

Andy Stanley tells the story of two young boys who go with their family on a camping trip to the beach. Dad parks the RV, mom starts supper, and the boys rush off to play in the surf until suppertime. For the next hour, they splash, wrestle, and sputter together, until one boy happens to look up and notice that the RV has vanished.

Panicking, the two boys run out of the water calling, "Daaaaaaad! Moooooom!" They wander down the beach, growing more and more frightened, when the little brother shouts "Hey! There it is! There's the RV!" They break into a sprint, eager to find their parents.

"Dad, why'd you move the RV? You should have told us you were changing camping spots!"

"I didn't change camping spots," Dad says, confused but insistent.

"But we played and played, and then when we looked up, the RV was gone! How did it change places if you didn't move it?"

Dad starts laughing. "Boys, we're parked in the same exact spot. But as you played in the water, the gentle undertow pulled you farther and farther down the beach. You'd have noticed if you'd been paying attention. But you were so busy playing that you never realized you were drifting with the current."

Every little choice is like an ocean undertow, gradually drifting one way or another. Your choices are either building you into a stronger person brick by brick, or you're gradually drifting with the current until you wake up not even able to recognize yourself. The good news is that you can make a definitive choice to walk out of the surf and take control of your trajectory.

NO CHOICE IS NEUTRAL

Choices either develop or destroy. They build habits into identity—into the person you already are and someday will become.

There is no neutral choice. Ever.

There are big choices and little ones.

There are options that are moral, some that are immoral, and even a few that may be amoral. But none are neutral. The decisions we make on small things are never simply small things.

Every choice we make in our individual lives is writing our story and creating our own personal brand. An old-fashioned term for it would be your "reputation." If you cross that tiny ethical line today, it's easier to do it again tomorrow. Next week there'll be another line to cross, and you'll keep making those little choices until you wake up one day and you've morphed into a person who is comfortable with choices you wouldn't have dreamed of making one or five or ten years ago. Or worse, you now don't realize that the lines you're crossing even exist.

The decisions that we make on small things are not just small things. I'm not trying to make you feel battered by being yet another person telling you that you're not doing a good job. I'm telling you because the way your brain makes memories and habits is by doing the same thing over and over again. Your decisions are turning you into something because they are building some kind of habit. I'm not saying that all choices are moral, but that no choice is neutral.

Your choices are either turning you into a person who cares more or a person who cares less. They're turning you into a person who is authentic or a person who is opaque. They are turning you into a person who has a skeleton in the closet or a person who keeps that closet swept and cobweb free because you never have anything to hide—because you choose not to make any decision that you'd want to hide in the first place.

Every choice we make in our business and in our individual lives is creating a brand. No choice is too small to warrant stepping back and asking yourself: what brand, what habit, what persona is this creating? And is it consistent with a life dedicated to living only one face?

Today's choices are not crucial because you're making the biggest choice of your life today. They're crucial because the choices you make today, tomorrow, and the next day are going to turn you into a person who, one year from now, either will or will not recognize the opportunity to make the biggest choice of your life. If today you cross that line and you keep making small, possibly unethical choices, in a year's time when you face a choice that would feel like an incredible leap out of character right now, it will then just be one more little insignificant choice.

The road you travel making all those little choices right now will dictate whether future moral dilemmas even blip on your radar. By then, you won't even recognize that it is a decision to be made or not made, because of the trend of little choices that create new habits. This isn't merely a problem isolated among individual leaders. It's a human problem. Corporations are made up of humans; therefore, corporations experience the same thing on a larger scale.

This is why it's absolutely crucial to guard the little choices.

STOP KISSING FROGS

Leadership, both personally and in your industry, isn't a fairy tale.

When it comes to ethics, team management, and other crucial decision-making, an awful lot of leaders leave things to chance. Sort of like the princess who kisses an awful lot of frogs (or toads… or whatever they're called) and just hopes for the best.

But healthy corporate and client interaction doesn't typically happen by accident. In the real world, kissing frogs and hoping for the best is far more likely to leave you with a mouthful of warts than a dashing prince. As team leader or organizational figurehead, you don't have the luxury of relying on chance.

Maybe you've drafted strategic business plans and marketing plans and investment plans. But what about your strategy for decision-making itself? Do you even have one? Don't freak out if you don't. If you haven't already, this is a perfect time to put this book down and go online to www.SarahMcDugal.com/free-stuff/ to download and complete my free Executive Values Discovery exercise. This will help you articulate your core values and understand how they inform the identity and culture of your company.

There's no reason to keep on kissing frogs and hoping you'll figure it out. I want to offer a nearly foolproof framework for making decisions that won't come back to bite you. Use this strategy to make smart, solid choices.

Every.

Single.

Time.

TAKE YOUR OPTIONS TO COURT

Pretend with me for a moment that you could take every choice before a panel of advisors. At this court, King Will(power) sits in judgment over every decision. When he's in a good mood, he works closely with his four closest advisors.

These four advisors are called Conscience, Common Sense, Desire, and Identity. Each advisor requires a simple Yes or No answer to one single question. When all four respond unanimously, your path is clear.

1. **Conscience**—Is it right? (Is it fair, ethical, moral?)
2. **Common Sense**—Is it best? (For this situation, person, place, and time?)
3. **Desire**—Do I really want it? (And do I also want the consequences and ramifications this choice entails?)
4. **Identity**—Does this choice align with my core values? (Is it compatible with who I want to become?)

These four deceptively simple questions will make a profound difference in how you manage both your corporate and client relationships. Use these four questions to arrive at ethical yet savvy business choices that will serve to benefit your long-term vision while simultaneously strengthening your credibility. If you trust these advisors, you'll never be caught second-guessing the authenticity of your decisions again.

You always have a choice. You are ultimately in the driver's seat. No matter what other people do or say, your choices of how to act and react are your own. Stop hoping you kiss the right frog and instead take your decisions to King Will's court.

Note: An in-depth study of these concepts, by Lois Eggers, MA, can be found through the Common Sense Psychology Foundation, www.CSPFoundation.com. Used by permission.

CHAPTER 5

THE GIFT YOU HATE TO LOVE

Your smile is your logo, your personality is your business card, how others feel after an experience with you is your trademark.

—Jay Danzie

L egend has it that a team of Japanese automobile engineers once visited an American car factory to learn the "American way." As they toured the factory, they noticed something intriguing. When the automobiles were on the assembly line, after the doorframes went into the cars, someone had the very specific job of standing over the line with a mallet and tapping around the edges of each doorframe to make sure everything was correctly fitted in place.

Puzzled, the Japanese guests asked, "What is that person doing?" An American manager explained that this

45

was an important element of quality control—to be sure the doorframes were perfect and to make sure every car passed inspection. The Japanese were boggled that someone would be hired for such a task. They just shook their heads, uncomprehending.

The American asked, "Don't you have quality control inspectors in your Japanese plants to check the doorframes?"

They replied, "No, if our door frames weren't fitting perfectly every time, we would not hire someone to check them at the end of the line. Instead we would go back to the design process and correct the problem from the very beginning of the design. We would never hire someone to tap door frames with mallets at the end of the line, because we aim for perfection from the beginning of a design."

When we aim for excellence from the start of a project, or a production, or from the inception of launching a new business, we naturally eliminate much of the sloppiness that would later require painful critique and costly repairs or recalls. However, the key is in the way we handle painful critique when it does happen, despite placing a high value on excellence that determines the character and integrity of the team—and of you as the leader.

CRITICISM VS. FEEDBACK

Criticism stinks.

Nobody likes getting criticized. Nobody enjoys being told how they need to change, or improve, or grow. I know I certainly don't—not naturally, anyway. Of course, depending on your personality and temperament, you may greatly enjoy dishing criticism out to others. But that still probably doesn't mean you like being on the receiving end.

Here's the conundrum—without recognizing your weak spots, you're never going to grow past them. If you're blind to your flaws and foibles, they have zero chance of becoming your strengths. And if you're intentionally embracing that blindness, then you're choosing to stagnate instead of reaching for success.

So how can you, as a conscientious leader, balance the components of humility and vulnerability but still maintain control of your success and stay in charge of your company?

THREE KEYS TO GROWING PAST YOUR SCREW-UPS

1. Look at feedback as a gift.

As long as you—the leader—set an example of responding to criticism as a threat, the rest of your team will follow suit. Growth areas will stagnate or regress. Clients and customers will feel disregarded. Fellow team members will feel increasingly slighted. And when conflicts arise or there is a challenge in the delivery of your product or service, your team will have no reference point for how to absorb the fallout in a healthy and positive way.

However, if you model the perspective of seeing criticism as feedback, no matter how painful or unwelcome, then your team will begin to develop a greater capacity for excellence because they no longer ignore their greatest opportunities for growth. Your team meetings may get louder, because suddenly everyone has the freedom to say what they really think without fear of reprisal. But that's actually great, because the worst meetings are the ones where everyone nods their heads and then expresses their true opinions in the hallway later. The healthiest team meetings are the ones where the entire team is welcome to express unfettered perspectives, to disagree vehemently, to put it all out on the table, and then to know that the best possible result has been achieved. The best meetings are the ones where no one has anything left to say by the end, because all have communicated honestly.

Instead of taking negative news as criticism, think of it as feedback. According to Lisa Sun, CEO of *Project Gravitas*, viewing criticism as feedback is the key to sustainable growth—both personally and corporately. "Criticism instinctively brings a sense of recoil, of being attacked," she says. "Feedback is information you can use to grow and change and develop new strengths. Feedback is a priceless gift."

2. Acknowledge that the sum of your team is greater than its parts.
And that includes accepting the (sometimes very difficult) fact that your team together is more valuable than you. Together, a good team makes magic that no individual member could create alone. It's humbling, but crucial, to consider the reality that your team is stronger and more powerful as a group because each person brings their specific set of skills, their own brilliance, their own perspective and worldview. When you combine those strengths together, working collaboratively in an ethical, respectful way, your results will be infinitely better. When you model honesty and transparency and recognize that each person on your team possesses giftedness in areas that are not yours, you empower your team to thrive.

One of the hardest things to do as a leader is to remember that you hired them because they're great at something you aren't. So get out of the way and let them be the expert in their niche. In my own branding and media production team, that means I have to step back from controlling and micromanaging what is not my area of giftedness or my particular skill, because micromanaging is not my role as team leader. My job is to inspire and hold each of my people accountable to do their best on behalf of the team and to accept their feedback when they come to me and say, "You know what, I think that we should do this over here, instead of what you suggested we should do. If you look at our goal, then doing it differently than the current plan is actually going to get us where we need to go."

If I want to be a strong, effective leader, I need to listen to their input, and I need to measure that input against their level of expertise. I also have to choose to trust my crew and know they are people of conscience who would not come and contradict me callously or without a good reason to suggest change. I need to be humble enough to accept that, because a big part of what makes my own team amazing is that they have the confidence to come and argue with me when they feel something is important.

3. Embrace vulnerability.

Embracing feedback requires vulnerability. Vulnerability is the opposite of what most leaders think they need to develop. Nobody tells you in business school to be more vulnerable. When you launch out as an entrepreneur, your mentors are far more likely to urge you to grow thick skin so you can shake off all the criticism that's headed your way than to encourage you to cultivate a spirit of humility.

That doesn't mean you are going to accept every single piece of feedback as an accurate reflection of the situation. But it does mean you need to reject arrogance long enough to give it due consideration, ponder the opportunities for growth that this information offers, and implement whatever has potential for positive change. Sometimes you may need to step back and chew on it for a few days before responding. Other times, it may cause an immediate and obvious shift in how your team operates.

Whatever the result, modeling a personal example of humility and vulnerability to feedback will set the tone of your team, your company, and your entire corporate brand. Combine that essence with a reputation for excellence, and you have the recipe for unstoppable success in the palm of your hand.

DEMAND THE EXTRAORDINARY

Strive for excellent. Demand extraordinary.

Excellence may be difficult at times, but being extraordinary is relatively easy. Why? Because society is filled with mediocrity. Excellence requires attention to detail, follow-through, organization, structure, and vision. Being extraordinary simply requires respectful attention to people.

Excellence is the goal, but you're guaranteed to sometimes fall short. Issues arise, problems crop up, stuff happens. No business is going to be able to maintain a perfect customer service record without ever encountering circumstantial difficulties or human error.

Obviously, there are fewer problems when excellence is the collective goal, or when a culture of excellence is already in place. But the extraordinary is proven in how those challenges are handled. When issues arise, you can either join the rest of the world in mediocrity by blowing it off or blaming the disgruntled customer or the under-performing team member. Or you can respond with a simple but unforgettable attitude of excellence.

"There's a problem? We're going to accept that feedback as deeply valuable. We're going to take it the extra mile. We're going to go double-check everything potentially related to this issue because we're honest like that, because we stand behind our product like that, because that's just who we are. We're not going to think twice about the extra effort because we know our core values."

All of a sudden, you are undeniably in a stratosphere above everyone else who would prioritize the status quo and reject feedback or respond defensively to the perceived threat of criticism.

CREATE AN ASSESSMENT CULTURE

Accepting assessment is important, but it isn't enough. Strong leaders move beyond personal assessment to promote, embrace, and encourage it as a staple of their corporate or team culture. They not only model vulnerability, but they also expect it and mentor it among those around them.

Vulnerable, values-driven assessment is largely absent in many levels of business structure; although the corporate world embraces it more than the non-profit or charity world does. That's primarily because the corporate world is more intensely focused on their bottom line and is willing to accept feedback if it will improve profits. However, that does not mean corporate teams automatically have a healthy structure of accepting feedback. Embracing critique for the purpose of bettering the bottom line is not at all the same as vulnerably embracing feedback for the greater purpose of overall, values-driven growth.

Non-profits and charities, in contrast, tend to avoid feedback and assessment at all costs. Since they don't have a profit margin to manage, they tend to view themselves as needing to focus entirely on the vision without paying attention to structure or process or a culture of improvement. As a result, they limit themselves in what they could become because they are not willing to hear how they could improve. If you lead in the non-profit or charity sphere and you're reading this, I hope this chapter will inspire you to step outside that status quo and model significant change.

CONVERSATIONS | LISA SUN | PROJECT GRAVITAS

If you've checked out any of my social media feeds in the process of reading this book, you'll already know that I love following and sharing companies that are crushing it in their sphere—the ones doing something amazing and doing it with flair.

Project Gravitas is one of these. My mother stumbled on their website and sent it to me, saying, "You'll love this!" She knows me well.

Last year for my birthday, my husband said, "What do you want?"

"A little black dress from *Project Gravitas*!" I said.

"What's so special about them?" he asked.

"Hah! Made in New York, by women, for women, top quality, Italian fabrics, and they emphasize social responsibility by giving back to charities every month—what's not to love?!"

Several Twitter exchanges and one ah-mazing little black dress later, I had the distinct privilege of spending an hour interviewing Lisa Sun, CEO, on the unique perspective *Project Gravitas* places on the value of accepting feedback. Susanna Hamilton, Marketing Director, sat in on the interview.

Sarah: I'm absolutely delighted that you would both take your time out to talk to me. I love your clothes. I love the premise behind your product. I love your message and story. Please share with me (and my readers!) more about your values and philosophy.

Lisa: When I started the company—before we launched—we had a vision board. We asked "In five years, what do you want to be able to say about this company?" And my Post-It note, which is still over my desk, said that my dream was for us to be a part of women's lives, to have impact, to be part of their story when they have a birthday, when they have an anniversary—that we would share a part in those moments.

Sarah: You mean, like me telling my husband that the only thing I want for my birthday is one of your little black dresses? And then wearing it so often that all my other clothes get neglected?

Lisa: Yes! This re-energizes me about why we do what we do. I don't do anything for financial gain, and I think if we do the right things, we will meet great women along the way. I'm moved hearing your story and so honored that you're taking the time to talk to us.

Sarah: It's mutual! I am working on this book about values-driven leadership, especially as it applies to branding, and the premise is that you cannot have multiple sets of core values that govern your different environments in life. You shouldn't be cutthroat and ruthless in one part of life and then pretend to be extremely ethical and a saint in another part of life. Just own who you are and do your best to live to that level of values. Whatever those values are, state them clearly and work constantly to be true to those. I believe sustainability in business, as well as in friendships and relationships, is best achieved by honesty and integrity, by acting in ethically responsible ways.

Lisa: We must be sharing the same brain wavelength, or you were at dinner last night with my group of investors! When I started this company, anybody who knows me well knows that *Project Gravitas* is essentially me—my values and philosophy. This is simply how I live.

If you order a dress from us or ask for a recommendation on which dress would best fit your body type and we don't get it right, then I believe we should tell you we didn't get it right and then we should help you find the right dress.

Embracing a level of vulnerability to acknowledge when you're wrong is part of the next wave of leadership. I tell my team, "If you're not vulnerable, if you can't admit when you need help—and that's me included—then you can't own your moment."

You cannot reach great heights until you've seen the valley, until you've put it out there, until you've addressed your challenges.

Sarah: *Project Gravitas* as a company was actually born out of one of those vulnerable moments in your personal experience, right?

Lisa: I was 22 years old when my first boss gave me some pretty crushing feedback. She's one of our angel investors now, so don't go and assume she is a terrible human being! But she said, "Lisa, you don't have any gravitas. Go buy a new dress, get some big jewelry, and wear great shoes."

Probably because of the environment I was from, I said, "That's so superficial! Do you really want me to go buy new clothes? I'm not making a lot of money to go waste on a new dress and shoes."

And she said, "You're the first person you have to look at in the mirror each morning. If you feel good about yourself, you're gonna carry that confidence throughout your day. So no, it's not superficial."

Sarah: That must have been a hugely vulnerable experience. But look at how you embraced that feedback and later launched a wildly successful company built around it.

Lisa: I always tell my team, "Our entire company was founded on a single piece of feedback. So when customers give us their own feedback, when our teammates offer feedback, we must be open to it, vulnerable to it, and then figure out how to do something positive with it. Vulnerability allows us to admit mistakes, correct them, and see them as opportunities to improve what we do.

Sarah: So you place a premium value on cultivating an openness to feedback, a humility toward critique, and the awareness that failures can be launching points to do things better instead of allowing them to crush you.

When I work with any company for branding, I sit with them to go through an Executive Values Discovery exercise. Do you have clearly defined values at *Project Gravitas* that everybody knows about?

Lisa: When I started the company, I wrote down six values— six things I believed—and stated that as we work with our partners, vendors, customers, anybody, this is how our company will make decisions. Then, our executive team rewrote the values together. When the CEO writes down values, it's one thing. But if you want the entire team to take ownership and internalize those values, they need to find their own language for how they express it. So I intentionally sought their involvement during the expression process.

Project Gravitas' resulting six core values are:

{Every Woman}

We believe in the beauty and power of women and want every woman to stand a little taller, have their "moment," and be remembered. We serve women of every size, shape, profession.

{This is Water}

We want to make a significant contribution by hearing the voices of the women we serve and providing them with beautiful pieces that fill their needs and provide lasting value. We are genuinely interested in solving problems. We deal fairly and meet customers and vendors more than halfway and with empathy.

{Patches of Sunshine}

We channel the flow—that current of mental energy that focuses our minds, motivates us to achieve, and generates happiness. This energy drives us to set aggressive goals and exceed them.

{Uncompromising Passion for New and Needed Products}

We believe in creating products that are visionary and necessary, products that will elevate women to achieve beyond their own expectations—and at a level of quality and value that earns the respect and loyalty of our customers. We accept the risks in pursuing bold visions.

{First Follower}

We believe great leaders inspire the next generation of leaders. The best leaders recognize the power of followership—"the first follower turns the lone nut into a leader." Mentorship, respect, and teamwork are at the heart of what we do.

{Our Life's Work}

This is not just a job—this is Our Life's Work. Our fingerprints and passion are woven into everything we do. We welcome everyone to be a part of this extraordinary adventure.

Sarah: Do you ever have situations where it is really difficult to stay true to these values?

Lisa: Oh yes. When these values are in conflict, it can be very painful trying to live them out. We just had a recent situation where we lived our values incredibly well, but it was absolutely not fun to do it. Three weeks ago a customer told us that a seam had come apart on the dress they purchased. We pulled all of the units of that style out of the warehouse, which was like two hours from our factory, and we inspected them again and re-stitched that seam on every single dress.

Sarah: Wow. So you didn't suggest that she bought the dress in a size that was too small for her, or that she should have taken better care of the dress, or imply that it was the customer's fault. Instead, you took the responsibility fully and then went on to make sure it never happened to anyone else.

Lisa: When there's a problem, I'm very grateful to our customers for letting us know, because maybe it says something about that style.

We resewed and reinforced the seam, and we did it on the entire inventory within 24 hours. And I totally panicked. I'm like, "Oh, my God! The seam could have been stronger; let me double stitch it up now!"

And my customer care director is amazing. I said, "Amy, email everyone who bought this style in the last four weeks." She checked in with every single customer to make sure they hadn't experienced the same issue. It's challenging to live true to our values when there's a crisis to avert, but I choose to believe we're really lucky that people care enough to email us and tell us.

Sarah: Your spirit of "thank you for telling us, now we're going to go pull every unit and triple-check everything at our own expense" is what makes people willing to tell you when they've found a problem. Because they know you're actually going to do something about it. And after that, even though there was a problem, they're likely to turn around and tell their girlfriends over coffee about this amazing company called *Project Gravitas*. "Hey girls, you know what? You gotta buy your next dress from them. I got one and loved it, and even though I had a problem with my seam, they fixed it and then totally went the extra mile."

Lisa: Exactly. That customer probably went to dinner with a friend and told her the story.

Sarah: And that's exactly what you want. Not a perfect record (although that would be nice!), but a reputation for responsible customer care that goes above and beyond.

Lisa: We have the mindset that feedback is a gift. Your best coaches are the ones who are the toughest, because they care enough about you to tell you. I always joke that if someone doesn't really care about you, they won't even take the time to give you feedback. They'll just let you continue on as you are. They have no vested interest in your growth. And so we view the customer, feedback and all, as a gift.

The second example I can give you is how we work as a team. We are good at what I like to call co-creating; I believe when people have their fingerprint on the answer, they feel more invested in the answer's success. So even the way we reshaped our corporate values together, that's been a co-creation process.

Susanna runs our company internship program, and our interns are really surprised when they get their four-week feedback session halfway through the summer. She will literally take each of them to coffee or breakfast and give them feedback. Here are the things that you are doing well. Here are the things you need to consider. And people are surprised we would make that level of investment in an intern.

Sarah: Wow.

Lisa: But from intern all the way up, each of us deserves feedback. Our screening process to become an intern is intensive, but once you are here our obligation is to give you the best professional experience possible. We believe that obligation includes bringing you into our corporate culture of strong feedback.

A personal example was last year, when one of my team members gave me tough feedback about how I was prioritizing my time. We all have a knee-jerk reaction, and I had to pause and say, "Wow, I really need to reflect on how I am spending my time." But what's exciting for me is that since I made that mental shift and took her feedback, there are a lot of things I am less involved in now. She's actually doing it better than I was. If this kind of corporate culture is going to work, then I think no one can be allowed to be immune to feedback—even the CEO.

Susanna: This was my second job out of college, and I had never worked somewhere where I got feedback before. I remember my first day in the office I was running a conference call between our warehouse and our factory, and I was in way over my head. Lisa took me out afterwards, and she said, "Here's what you did well, here's a tip to do better." That stuck with me. From day one, I realized what I could expect here at *Project Gravitas* and that this would be a professional development experience because that was how we looked at feedback here.

Sarah: Now that leads me to a question. You've talked a lot about creating a culture where critique is both expected and embraced, and where people feel they are free to give feedback that may be hard for the other person to hear. It seems to me that people need to know their job is not on the line just because they are receiving critical feedback.

Do you have processes in place where there is a certain number of times someone gets to tell you, "You need to improve on this specific thing," before it becomes an issue for your employment? How do you make sure people are not afraid of being fired or demoted just because you have this openness to clearly address issues for the sake of improvement?

Lisa: We do have a formal annual feedback process. We've only had one situation where the feedback had led to someone leaving the company. We front-load a lot of the hiring process so that expectations are extremely clear from the beginning. We say look, "You jumped through a lot of hoops to get here, so therefore we trust you and believe in you, and we want to see you grow. So let us give you opportunities where you can grow. Part of that will be making mistakes; part of that will be correcting mistakes." If we bring the right people in and make that hiring process rigorous up-front, then you don't worry about losing your job because you know we are invested in your success. You see feedback truly as a gift, and you are given opportunities to show how you accept that feedback and how you act on it.

I remember Suze's first day too. I gave her feedback on the conference call she had struggled with, and ever since then she has been on top of it. I think throughout the process I'm pretty open with someone when I say, "Look, this is because I care about you and want to take you to the next level."

Sarah: How do you eliminate the catty environment that often results from having a lot of women working together in close quarters? I'll be honest, I often find it much easier to work with men despite chauvinism and sexism and the good ol' boy's club, because oftentimes women are so jealous and gossipy and backstabbing.

Lisa: Oh yeah. One of my mentors taught me, "Groups of women can either become really catty, or they can become really supportive and help each other." I asked "What's the difference between the two groups?" She said, "It depends on the person at the top, whether or not there is a competitive sense of who is the favorite. You can't have favorites. And you have to believe that you all rise above together. All ships will rise in the tide." If we get competitive or catty or seeking recognition, then we have lost sight of what matters, which is making customers really happy and having fun while we're doing it.

It also helps to make sure there are clear boundaries drawn around who is responsible for what and who gets the resulting credit for what. Clearly define ownership of different duties.

Sarah: That's very quotable. To distill what you've said so far:

clearly know your values,

- show vulnerability,
- willingly embrace feedback even if that means you need to step back and process it,
- draw clear boundaries of ownership and job roles, and
- give plenty of shared credit to other people on the team.

Lisa: I think that sums it up well!

CHAPTER 6

ONE FACE

When our private internal identity matches our external identity, we have the power of authenticity and integrity at our disposal.

—Jane E. Stevenson

I threw up the entire time I was pregnant. Both times around. With my first child, I had to stop driving because I kept blacking out behind the wheel. With my second child, complications landed me in the High Risk Antenatal Unit on weeks of bed rest. I'd find myself hugging the toilet until I thought I'd puked my toenails up. People would ask, "Are you okay, honey?" Because my eyes were so bloodshot from violently vomiting. And also because we lived in Atlanta, Georgia, where random strangers still call pregnant women "honey."

My hormones and emotions went crazy, and I felt completely out of control. I'm not talking normal pregnancy mood swings. I'm talking deep, dark depression. Blackness that pulled me down so low I wondered if life was still worth it.

For months during my first pregnancy, I teetered on the edge of an emotional abyss.

Part of my challenge was caused by my very rigid and narrowly defined idea of "good motherhood." Good mothers never work outside the home. They don't travel the world or let anyone but the grandparents babysit. They abandon all personal interests. Good mothers pour every waking thought and dream and shred of energy into nothing but forming the characters of their children.

Right?

I felt like my identity was a rug being yanked out from under my feet. Without the collaborative team I'd invested in for the previous several years, I didn't know who I was or who I could become.

I also didn't realize that much of my depression was chemical. I'd never before encountered an emotional obstacle I couldn't conquer with "mind over matter." It didn't help that my severe insomnia kept me awake day and night. I often clocked less than 8 hours of sleep in a week.

My family worried about the baby's health because I was uncharacteristically morose, but they had no idea what a mess I was inside. I didn't have the courage to tell my husband either, and every night I would lie awake jealously listening to him sleep, while a vicious cycle of negative mental talk dragged me deeper into despair.

"I'll never be able to work with an amazing production team again, because now I will be a mother."

"I'm not ready to become a mother."

"I hate myself for not being thrilled about this gift of life."

"What kind of awful woman doesn't want to be a mother?"

"If I'm honest with my friends about this, will they still love me?"

I battled all these emotions, and then battled shame for feeling them in the first place. No matter how hard I tried, I couldn't "snap out of it." Six weeks before my son was born, I finally opened up to my husband. Anger, desperation, and discouragement poured out, and he listened beautifully.

Then he asked why I'd carried this weight alone for so long. Why?

Because most of my adult life I'd been terrified of displeasing others. Because I didn't want to let people down. Because I was ashamed. Because I was angry that those who loved me hadn't figured it out and stepped in to help me already. Because, although my core values were strong, I'd never owned them enough to release my fear of judgment by onlookers.

Because I wanted to be liked more than I wanted to lead.

Then, one late fall morning, he arrived. This 7 pound 12 ounce, olive brown bundle, with clear gray eyes and a Kewpie doll fauxhawk, staring at me like he was soaking up the world's genius with every waking moment.

They laid him on my chest in the operating room, and I was mush. I stared at him, as new mothers do, checking every miniature finger and marveling at this tiny person who had turned my life upside down but hadn't seemed real just 10 minutes before.

My fear of anyone else's judgment evaporated. With vivid clarity, I knew that I would never give outside opinions quite the same weight again.

I parent differently than you? No problem.

My house isn't as fancy as yours? Big deal.

You hold a contrary opinion? Lucky for you, it's a free country.

I don't mean to sound intentionally snarky or combative. I just didn't care about peripherals any more.

For the first time in my life, oddly combined with the period of deepest exhaustion and sleep loss, I felt utterly free. There were only three sources that mattered—my conscience before God, my relationships at home, and doing right by our innocent child. If something didn't directly affect those or the projects I'd chosen to accomplish for clients, it wasn't worth the energy loss.

Living with one face brings freedom. You're not losing sleep over keeping people happy or keeping secrets hidden. When you live with transparency, there's no need to put on an "act" because your whole life is already in line with your values.

SLEEP ON WINDY NIGHTS

As a child, my parents often told me a classic children's tale about a boy who wanted a job working on a farm. This boy comes up to a farmer who's advertising for a young hired hand. He's just a kid, maybe 12 or 13 years old. The farmer asks, "What are your qualifications, son?"

The boy replies, "I can sleep on windy nights."

"What is that supposed to mean?" the farmer asks.

"It means, sir, that I can sleep on windy nights," the boy replies.

Not sure what to make of it, the farmer decides to take a chance and hire the kid anyway. Things go along fine for a while. The boy seems to do his job well and never complains. The farmer starts to feel comfortable, although he still wonders sometimes what that nonsense about windy nights was about.

Then one night, a huge thunderstorm rolls in. The farmer wakes up in a panic. He races out into the wind and the rain, absolutely certain his haystacks are already blowing away, that the shed door needs to be latched, that the animals will be scattered from their pens. He storms into the bunkhouse to wake the boy, shakes him by the shoulders, and yells, "Get up! Get out and help me!"

The boy just mumbles in his sleep and rolls over. Exasperated, the farmer heads back out alone, planning to fire his lazy farmhand just as soon as the sun comes up.

He reaches the haystacks, and to his surprise, everything is intact. The tarps are securely tied and withstanding the thunderous onslaught. He stumbles to the barn, where every last stall is properly latched, and each animal is tethered as they should be. Bewildered at the fine state of his property, he checks the henhouse, the smokehouse, and the cellar doors. Every last one is as tightly shuttered as if he had done it himself.

And suddenly he knows exactly what the boy meant when he said, "I can sleep on windy nights." This kid was so sure of himself, not in a cocky or disrespectful way, but so completely confident that he didn't have anything to prove. He knew his values, and he was at peace with his integrity. He could sleep on windy nights because he didn't wait for a storm to come before he did his job properly. Instead, he did the right thing all the time. He could still sleep on windy nights because that was his ethic.

When you live that way, it takes all the pressure off. You don't have to juggle different identities—because you're only living one.

QUIT FAKING ALREADY

The restaurant industry probably has one of the smallest margins for error in achieving customer satisfaction. Food either tastes good, or it doesn't. Your meal arrives hot and on time, or it doesn't.

But when you move into the area of sustainability, things can get murky. It's dangerous, no matter the industry, to pretend to be one thing for PR's sake if it's not really who you are.

In late 2014, *Chipotle* got the chance to decide how to act with integrity. Upon discovering that one of their pork suppliers was violating animal treatment standards, the restaurant chain pulled all pork from its menu at hundreds of locations. This got a lot of mileage in good will from the animal rights side and reinforced that the company was truly dedicated to sustainable meat-sourcing and not just pretending.

"We'd rather not serve pork at all, than serve pork from animals that are raised in this way," spokesman Chris Arnold said to Business Insider. *Chipotle's* website stated, "When sourcing meat, we work hard to find farmers and ranchers who are doing things the right way."

In early 2015, *Chipotle* continued its health-conscious trend by announcing the removal of all genetically modified (GMO) ingredients from its menu, stating that GMO products don't align with its slogan of offering "food with integrity."

I had a chance to spend an hour with Monty Moran, co-CEO of *Chipotle*, chatting about the values that drive their leadership and vision. I started by asking his opinion on the most common objection I hear from business people about leading with integrity: "There's no way you can be wildly successful in business without cutting corners!"

"That's absolute unmitigated horse manure," Monty said. "I don't know how you can succeed *without* living the same face both directions. I suppose it might be possible, but I don't believe it really happens. Not in the long haul. It can't create a sustainable culture.

So how does Chipotle achieve such a values-driven corporate culture despite the explosive growth they've experienced in the past few years?

When we hire, we don't care about experience at all. Instead, we hire people who display a set of 13 characteristics, which I came up with, that I do not believe can be taught. You either have them or you don't.

Hire people for character, and you have a better chance of getting people who can be sensitive, open, understanding, and caring about the people around them. After getting hired, our foundational principle is that *each person will be judged and rewarded based on their effectiveness in making the people around themselves better*. That drives everything we do—how we compensate, who becomes our future executives, whom we exalt and hold up as examples of great leaders.

When I started, less than 20% of our employees made it from crew to manager. Now, nearly all of our general managers come up from within the crew. First you hire fantastic people, then you reward people based on their effectiveness in making others better. And when they do, you make heroes out of them, you announce it, you promote them. You celebrate the success of making others better, and what happens is a multifold win.

First, you get lots of people being developed. Second, people start to realize what it means to care about and empower somebody outside of themselves. To be a *Chipotle restaurateur*, our elite general manager position, you must have a team of top performers who are empowered to achieve high standards. So, there are three criteria: top performers, empowerment, and high standards. High standards are a throwaway because if you have top performers who are empowered with the right kind of knowledge, high standards are gonna fall out the bottom like a vending machine.

How do you build a crew of all top performers? First, you hire for character. Second, you teach that the path to success is to make people around you better. A top performer is someone who *has the desire and ability to perform excellent work* and through their constant effort to do so, *elevates themselves, the people around themselves, and Chipotle.*

So there are two parts to the definition: 1) do a great job and 2) make others better. Doing a great job isn't enough to make you a top performer. You have to do a good job *and* make others better, and do it all of the time.

Monty Moran's management philosophy works not only because it is driven by values and a strong focus on character, but also because *Chipotle's* executive leadership has taken the time and energy to focus clearly on discovering and articulating the values that matter to them. Instead of obsessing solely on their bottom line, they've taken the long-range perspective and are willing to cut losses in the short-term if it means they'll have greater integrity in the end. This commitment to development, empowerment, and their own people has a profound positive impact on their potential for longevity.

BACK TO THE DRAWING BOARD

Consider *Hampton Creek Foods*, another company that leads the food industry and has built an entire corporate culture based on a clear set of values. Launched in 2013, by the summer of 2014, *Hampton Creek* had been named as 36th on CNBC's Disruptor 50 list and described by Jim Cramer as one of the top companies that are "shaking up the status quo and have the potential to be … future public powerhouses. *Hampton Creek* has answered the age-old question 'what came first, the chicken or the egg?' by taking the chicken out of the egg, with its plant-based egg substitute."

Within 10 months of showing up on the shelves, *Hampton's* vegan product Just Mayo was already the best-selling brand of mayonnaise in Whole Foods. By early 2015, the entrepreneur and tech design magazine Fast Company had named *Hampton Creek* as number two on "The World's Top 10 Most Innovative Companies of 2015 in Food."

Hampton Creek makes the bold claim that they are in the "pursuit of making eggs obsolete and making healthy food more affordable. Making it easier for regular people to do the right thing," says Josh Tetrick, *Hampton Creek's* founder and CEO. "We're in Costco and Safeway and the Dollar Tree. It's about accessibility. Good food shouldn't just be for people who make six figures. It should be for everyone."

Hampton Creek has decided that in order to manufacture and sell an egg-free product, it has to taste just as good or better than the real deal, it has to be sustainably sourced from organic and non-GMO ingredients, and it has to be able to sell at the same price point as its junk food counterpart. As their brand manager, Jordan Viola, told me in this chapter's case study interview, "If we can't find a way to meet all three requirements, the product goes back to the drawing board."

CONVERSATIONS | JORDAN VIOLA | HAMPTON CREEK FOODS

I never dreamed *Hampton Creek Foods* would actually respond to my unsolicited query for an interview. But within 10 minutes of my email through their web portal, a reply popped into my inbox. A few days later, I found myself on the phone with Jordan Viola. Obviously a man of action, he stepped out of his office to walk as we talked.

Sarah: Who determines your company's vision?

Jordan: I work very closely with our CEO, Josh Tetrick, on messaging, branding, everything about the *Hampton Creek* brand. Together we determine what we stand for, what we look like to the outside world. We carve out the image and the brand. We realized early on that the two of us collaborating was so much more effective than outsourcing to someone sitting outside the office. We're able to create on the spot, in-house with people who enthusiastically understand the meaning, the purpose, and the why behind what we do. With a small team who shares clearly unified values, you can be twice as effective if your people understand that—to hijack Apple's mantra—"a million No's lead up to one awesome Yes."

We constantly ask ourselves: if we started over right now, how would we be clever? How would we be unique? How would we be fun and approachable and accessible to everyone, everywhere? That attitude has allowed us to explore consistent branding, consistent story ideas, across all of our mediums. Doesn't matter if it's Facebook, or a simple message to in-store customers, or a demo.

Sarah: How do you effectively make *Hampton's* brand personality and values consistent across all platforms—product, service, social media? In an average company, it's very rare for so many parallel platforms to be as unified and cohesive as *Hampton Creek's*. I'm impressed, not just as a consumer, but as a fellow branding professional looking from the outside and admiring your work.

Jordan: That's very kind of you! Think about pitching a product, in terms of why your product is better or different. You can talk all day about health benefits, non-GMO, sustainability.

Sarah: Right, but that's all facts and data, which are totally forgettable.

Jordan: Yes. What it really came down to for us is this: if we are going to be a food company that is really going to make a difference, then it's more important than anything for our product to just taste good. The product itself needs to be consistent across the board. Taste is a human experience, not focused on what the product is doing or delivering. It's how that person reacts, and how that person thinks about it.

We ask ourselves: will my mom like this? Will my aunt like this? Will my brother in Brooklyn connect with this? Is my grandma who lives on Long Island going to connect with this? What about my uncle who has cholesterol problems?

Of course we have a centralized core message that we believe in—health, sustainability, making a difference in the world. Then we have the next layer that is all about "This tastes delicious, and it's good for you!" We don't necessarily touch on all specific health or sustainability benefits, but we say, "It's better for you and better for the planet."

Then on the outer layer is the idea of being clever and unique. Trying to avoid clichés, telling the story differently than in the past. We look for influence and inspiration outside the food world, too. If you get too focused and tunnel visioned about a product and its quality, you get lost, and the storytelling piece becomes totally disconnected. It loses consistency. We check the status quo and then try to go as far in the opposite direction as we can. And all the time bringing it back to the main focus—we are a human-centric product, offering a human experience. This propels our mission from day to day to day.

Sarah: I think you guys have absolutely achieved that. When I look at everything else on the grocery store shelf, you stand out, like the Apple of health food brands, if I were to compare you. If I understand correctly, you're not just telling the story of the product; you're telling the stories of all the people who engage with it.

Jordan: Absolutely. We realize that, from a design standpoint, brand loyalty is huge. People buy clothing and products because of the brand name. It might be the worst quality in the food world, but they buy what they are comfortable with. We want to help people think differently and innovatively in terms of what they are eating. We want them to realize that in the long run it makes a huge difference, not only for you, but for a hundred million people all over the world.

Sarah: In other words, you aren't merely telling the story of your product and your company. You're also not just telling the story of people who engage with the product. You are doing something much bigger. You're inviting them to...

Jordan: To be a part of the journey of *Hampton Creek.*

Sarah: ...and to join you in actually changing their story.

Jordan: I hate this word, but we are trying to invoke a sense of empowerment among people. What happens in design and creative and marketing is basically just an ability to create a connection in relationships. We see the entire world as a constellation of relationships.

So it comes back to the products we create, the message we tell. But underneath that, we are trying to share the story of *Hampton Creek* outside of the actual product. We want to create more of a movement, an entire revolution moving forward about the ideals that really support the product behind the scenes. It's all about the deeper message that's driven by our values.

Sarah: It's obvious that your corporate values drive the production and research process for your products, but how do those values translate into marketing and social media?

Jordan: For starters, not blasting low-quality content! Also, treating social media no differently than if we were creating a marketing campaign to sell Just Mayo. It's seeing those moments and really being able to seize them and take advantage of them. People respond well to the approach and the concept of what we're building. The more we can leverage the human-centric focus, I think the more and more it will grow. At the end of the day, a product is just a product.

If there's no deeper why attached to it, then you are going to lose in the long run.

CHAPTER 7

FRAMED

I would prefer even to fail with honor than to win by cheating.

—Sophocles

D r. Ben Carson was a childhood hero of mine. He grew up in extreme poverty, with an unquenchable drive to learn. At least, that's what his mother had in mind for him until the dream became his own. As a young man, he studied medicine and became a world-renowned neurosurgeon, the first to successfully separate conjoined Siamese twins. He changed the lives of countless people through his "Gifted Hands" as he led neurosurgery at Johns Hopkins.

He's so legendary that Cuba Gooding, Jr., played him in a feature-length film. For many fans, Dr. Ben Carson is an institution, a brand unto himself. Later in life, he became increasingly involved in politics and wrote an article in the Washington Times about cleaning skeletons out of the closet.

During his tenure at Johns Hopkins, a woman from Florida accused him of fathering her son. She sued for a paternity test, which Dr. Carson emphatically declined. Eventually the suit was dropped without further charges, but it doesn't sound like he lost a lot of sleep over the accusation. Dr. Carson says, "What she didn't know is that I did not have to scratch my head and try to remember which affair she represented, because I knew that the only woman I have ever slept with in my life was my wife."

While it was undoubtedly frustrating and inconvenient to be falsely accused, Dr. Carson knew he had nothing to hide and nothing to cover up. There was no skeleton to be found in that closet, because he knew he had lived true to his values.

Whether you're a young farm hand or a world-famous neurosurgeon, there's a lot of comfort to be found in a clear conscience.

Life is less stressful when you have no skeletons stashed in the closet. There's nothing to spin, no lies to keep track of. But what about when you do what is right and you're still wrongly perceived? How can you live with one face when you made the honorable choice, but everyone thinks you're guilty? Is it possible to maintain your integrity even when you're falsely accused?

DISCOVERING GENUINE FULFILLMENT

Orlando "Bo" Bowen was on top of the world. After a successful stint in the corporate world, Bo was recruited to play professional football.

The child of immigrant parents, Bo knew what hunger felt like. He knew what extreme poverty meant. And he was absolutely determined to overcome the odds. Getting an education was his best shot at never feeling cold or hungry again, so college became his all-consuming goal. "I never, ever wanted to depend on government assistance for food, shelter, and clothing again," he says.

As Bo grew up, he just knew that educational and financial independence would bring happiness and fulfillment. Two prestigious degrees later, he launched a career in IT and was making great money. "I'd thought I would feel this euphoric sense of self-actualization with everything I'd accomplished, but I didn't," he says. And then he took a trip back home to Jamaica. In his own words:

> At my friend's wedding back in Jamaica, I encountered a young boy begging for a couple of dollars so he could get a piece of bread. I thought I'd accomplished a lot in life at that time, but here was this kid asking for was money so he can get basic food. I thought to myself, "What have I really accomplished? There's so much more I can do. So much more I need to do."
>
> I decided that day to do what I could, to give back not only through my own physical resources, but also through sharing the life experiences I'd gained to that point. I wanted to help this boy, and young men like him, fend for themselves.
>
> So I took him to get something to eat, but it felt like I was just putting a Band-Aid over a severed limb.

I returned home to Chicago thinking, "Okay, we've gotta do something about this!" and started recruiting people in my old company to begin creating a mentorship program.

That's when I got a call from the Toronto Argonauts, with the Canadian Football League, inviting me to try out for the team. I had one burning question: "Will I have the opportunity to serve others if I make the team?" That was more important than anything else to me at the time. That was where my values were—I was tired of making money for its own sake. I wanted to be doing good with how I'd been gifted.

The Argonauts promised that if I made the team, I would have opportunities to serve, so I took a pay cut and left corporate America for the opportunity to give back.

After making the team, I immediately got involved in the community hoping to make a difference and ended up volunteering with a number of different organizations: training police, working with kids, running leadership programs, and serving as a celebrity liaison between law enforcement and the local communities, seeking to bring both sides together against racism.

I was excited about the chance to empower others through my journey, with whatever resources I had.

ASSAULTED AND FRAMED

Bo married Skye, a schoolteacher, and they started a family. A little boy was born, and by the time he was a year old, they were expecting a second son. Life was good. And then one evening, Bo was assaulted by the police.

He'd just signed a contract for his fifth year as a pro athlete and went out to dinner with friends to celebrate. Skye stayed home to put their son to bed early. Waiting by his car in the restaurant parking lot for his friends to arrive, Bo was talking on the phone when two undercover policemen approached him and initiated an altercation. Before he knew what was happening, Bo was savagely beaten.

Lying there, blood streaming down his face, mouth filled with asphalt, he believed he was going to die that night. The thought that filled his mind was, "God, I still have more to give back."

Unrecognizable from his injuries and handcuffed in the back of the squad car, a backup officer checked Bo's ID and was horrified to discover they'd just assaulted the CFL liaison to their own police force. In fact, he was scheduled to be the keynote speaker at a joint police-community event called *The Race Against Racism* in just a few days.

On the spot, a cover-up ensued to frame Bo for drug-dealing. The officers planted cocaine on the scene and accused him of assaulting them first.

Bo and Skye lost everything. A severe concussion and other injuries forced him to quit the team. Friends abandoned them. Colleagues shunned him. He faced agonizing months of legal proceedings before the investigation established that his assailants were running a corrupt drug ring within the police force, and they were sent to prison.

"I'd been talking about making a difference, about building into young people and bridging the gap between police and community. I'd been talking about overcoming racism and judgment on both sides, but I never dreamed my life would become Exhibit A in the process," Bo says.

Friends urged them to keep a low profile until it was sorted out. Family begged them to get away and take some time off. "I kept thinking 'But why? I'm not going to leave just because it's hard. I'm not gonna run away just because my apple cart has been upset. We have work to do—that's the whole reason I came here in the first place!'"

His keynote speech invitation was rescinded, but he and Skye went to *The Race Against Racism* anyway. The police chief was there; the officers he'd worked alongside as a celebrity spokesperson were there. It was a space where he had once been celebrated, and now he would be treated as a villain. Bo says:

> My legs felt like jelly as I dressed for the event. My face hadn't fully healed yet from the assault. But this was a cause I believed in, despite what had just happened to me. I determined not to let the incident change my values. My value set maintained that we need to come together as a community. I was still convinced we needed to bridge the gap between community and law enforcement, so we could be the best community possible.
>
> I had to ask myself, "What is my role in this?" Even if I wasn't going to be the keynote speaker, even if there

were folks who didn't want me there—it wasn't about them. I'd gotten a lot of heat from the black community for being involved with police relations. A lot of folks would say, "You know they don't respect us; you know they're always after us. They are always doing things to us." It made no sense to them why I would voluntarily work with law enforcement.

But things will never get better if we don't do something, and this was what I could do. What can you do if you see something that's not right? What can YOU do? It was about what I had come to Canada to do, and that was to serve. So we went.

My wife and I got in line where the Police Chief was signing autographs, and talking to attendees, and taking photos with everyone. We were the last ones. When he finished up with the couple in front of us, he looked at Skye and me and he put an arm around his colleague and turned and walked away.

Skye started crying. This man had been our friend. He'd played with my little son. It hurt, but I wasn't really surprised. The entire situation gave ammunition to those who believed I shouldn't have been trying to bring peace between the community and police anyway. They wanted me to abandon it and admit that I shouldn't be doing it in the first place. But I couldn't. I believed that the reason I was here on Earth was greater than the challenges we were facing. My faith insisted that God could use what had happened to me, in some way, to help somebody else.

A COMFORTING COMPASS

Even when you live and conduct your business consistently with integrity, there may be times when you are perceived wrongly, misunderstood, or outright falsely accused. Hard times teach the grueling lesson that living according to clearly defined values can be a comforting compass, even during seasons of injustice. Even if you've been falsely accused.

The danger comes from the temptation to abandon your values when you're desperate.

As a business or branding leader, this temptation can take many forms. When a dissatisfied customer tweets unfounded but vicious complaints about your company, how do you respond? Do you hotly defend your team's rightful actions? Do you tweet back with a snarky comment to put them in their place? Or do you apologize that they feel badly served and offer to make it right?

How you handle angry clients, misperceptions, and even false accusations speaks volumes about your commitment to the values that are supposedly driving your organization. Do the gloves come off, or do you maintain focus on acting honorably in all circumstances?

Ultimately, the goal is to be able to look yourself in the mirror at night and know that today's choices were in alignment with your core values, regardless of whether others understand or agree. In situations when you are misrepresented, the goal is to cling to your values, continue using your four advisors—Conscience, Common Sense, Desire, and Identity—to guide your decision-making process, and showcase the truth through your actions, without deviating.

CONVERSATIONS | ORLANDO BOWEN | ONE VOICE ONE TEAM

Orlando Bowen was fully acquitted, but his injuries made it impossible to return to professional football. Ten years after the assault, he wrote a public letter of forgiveness to his assailants. In 2005, he launched *One Voice One Team*, a youth leadership charity that has impacted 350,000 lives through presentations, workshops, summer camps, etc.

He is a motivational speaker on the subject of forgiveness and its direct connection to high performance—for audiences in the corporate world, law enforcement, and the military. *One Voice One Team* has garnered multiple awards, including the Queen Diamond Jubilee national award in Canada.

Sarah: Do you believe it is possible to be successful in business and still, as I like to put it, live with one face and maintain your integrity?

Orlando: Yes, I do. For some, it may seem like an oxymoron. Some people are convinced that you've got to put on a different face in order to be successful.

Sarah: Or cut corners, or sacrifice ethics, or…

Orlando: You know what? I've never subscribed to that. On the team, you know, cutting corners wasn't an option. Not because you could get away with it and no one might see, but because you would know in your heart.

Sarah: That was huge. Say that again?

Orlando: As an athlete, I learned that it was never about thinking, "Okay, I shouldn't cut corners because someone may see me." Or, "I shouldn't take a performance enhancing drug because I may get caught." It was about being able to look in the mirror and know you did all that you could, fair and square. I'd rather give everything I have fair and square and lose than cheat and win. I can't look myself in the mirror and sleep well knowing that I didn't do all that I could or that I cut corners or did something that was underhanded. That would be very difficult for me.

Sarah: If you could crystallize your top three pieces of advice, what would you say to someone who is feeling discouraged because they know they've done the right thing but they are facing some kind of injustice? Whether in the corporate world or in their personal life, they are trying to reconcile their right choice with the fact that they did not get a right reward. They got an unjust consequence when they did not deserve it. What would your advice be to them in the valley of that experience?

Orlando: First, I think it's important to surround yourself with others who share your value system, who support, encourage, and challenge you to hold steadfast to those values, whether things are going well or not. There's one thing guaranteed in life other than death and taxes, and it's that we're going to face challenges. Obstacles are just part of life. So knowing that, you can hold steadfast to the values that drive you. Knowing you did you right will carry so much weight for you and allow you to walk with your head high and shoulders tall. Acting honorably gives you the ability to weather the storm.

Sarah: So you're saying: stay the course and surround yourself with people who share an integrity-driven value system, instead of people who encourage you to cut corners in order to reduce the strain or the consequences or to "manage" the fallout.

Orlando: Correct.

Sarah: Is there a third? Or more? You can share more than three!

Orlando: The race isn't for the swift. Some people build their businesses and their lives on things that aren't true or authentic to them, and they will feel that eternal struggle. Seek out mentors who can give you long-term, big-picture perspective.

Sometimes a situation seems insurmountable in the moment, but wise mentors can remind you that other people made it through. Knowing that someone out there has survived what you are experiencing will help you remember that it is possible.

Sarah: Right. So, to summarize:

- stay the course,
- cultivate a network that shares your values,
- seek mentors who give wise perspective for the long haul.

Orlando: That sums it up well. I realize that my journey allows my family and I to connect with people who've had traumatic experiences on a whole different level. When I speak to audiences, it's actually God speaking through me. I'm just a conduit.

CHAPTER 8

U-TURN

No man, for any considerable period of time, can wear one face to himself and another to the multitude without finally getting bewildered as to which may be the truth.
—Nathaniel Hawthorne

I t's the little choices that sneak up on us, not the big ones. So what do you do if you wake up one morning with the uneasy realization that you have somehow drifted far from your original values? How do you rediscover integrity when you've lost sight of your compass? Is it ever too late to turn around?

The answer ultimately depends on how badly you want to sleep at night. Regardless of what the world may imply, when it comes to integrity, you always have a choice. No unethical action is fully thrust upon you without your involvement. If you're discouraged because you realize you haven't been living according to your values, don't lose hope. Yes, you may face challenging reconciliation personally or in business, but the risk is absolutely worth the clean conscience.

Let me tell you about my friend Holly.

Holly and I roomed down the hall from each other in college, and we quickly became best friends. Her multi-lingual fluency combined with her musical ability on several instruments dazzled me. We'd sprawl our literature books across the floor and study together, homework punctuated by hysterical laughter at some silly joke. We've now been friends for nearly two decades, often living hundreds of miles apart, always journeying closely together through the different but equally agonizing hands life has dealt to us both. Her anguish is directly related to surviving the fallout of life with someone who did not live with one face. That is, until she gathered the courage to make a turnaround.

Holly married young, to someone she believed to be a person of integrity. She thought his values aligned with hers and that he would be a positive spiritual influence. She wanted to live a life completely dedicated to her faith. She dreamed of adopting orphans and caring for the hurt and broken. She aspired toward visions of medical school and making a powerful difference in the world.

In her own words:

> I felt we would be a good complement to each other even though there were hints before we married that his character was not what I had assessed it to be. Other

people around us could see it, but I couldn't. We were married when I was just 20 years old. Soon after, I started to realize that what I had seen as his adherence to values was merely an outward attempt to convince himself and others, but underneath the façade, he wasn't who he said he was. In public he was religious to the point of sanctimonious. In private he was abusive to the point of violence, controlling and narcissistic, and an addict. There was no integrity there, no cohesion between what he said and who he was inside.

That lack of cohesion led to a very different reality in private life, behind closed doors, from whom he showed himself to be when we were out among people. And so the fallout for me really was that I started to lose my grasp on where I stood. It was like being in a spell, where the times I was actually coherent and remembered who I was and what I stood for seemed like sessions of madness. But then I would fall back under the spell. And that's how I lived my life for five years.

I had moments of clarity when I thought, "Oh my God, what am I doing here? What have I done? How can I get out of this?" But I would quickly fall back into despair thinking, "There's no way to get out. This is my reality." Over time, it became easier to just stay under the spell and do what I could to prevent another session of clarity so that I didn't have to actually face the fact that I was living in two completely different worlds.

After a while, Holly's dichotomy between the values she wanted to live and the values she found herself living created unbearable tension between who she wanted to be and who she felt trapped into being. She found herself denying the values that were most true to her, just to keep the stress manageable.

Whether we're talking about brands or companies or individual leaders, many people do not take the time to consider the amount of angst that living multiple faces brings into your life. Once you've brought yourself face to face with that tension, you have no choice but to take action. Until the pain of staying the same becomes greater than your fear of change, it may seem easier to lie to yourself than to face the tension and choose to be a person who you actually like in the mirror.

It's nice to hope that everyone has the ability to recognize when enough is enough and then authentically acknowledge the truth underneath. But, at least in the short term, it can be more appealing to carry on comfortably as we have been. Until we get to a point of forced change, it often feels easier to lie to ourselves than to get uncomfortable for the sake of improvement.

In Holly's experience, there were two things that pushed her to the point of embracing change. The first one was purely unselfish. Holly realized in a moment of clarity that this toxic relationship was going to permanently and negatively impact her infant daughter if she didn't change her example of how a woman should act in a parenting and marriage relationship.

Holly says:

I realized that I was basically non-functional in the rest of my life because of the conflict and the tension in those two roles with my then-husband. His toxic contempt for me became painfully obvious one night, when our toddler daughter woke up about 2 a.m. and wanted a refill on her sippy cup of water. I was in a deep sleep, and I kinda stumbled into the bathroom, turned the faucet on, and filled up her sippy.

Her father woke up and saw that I'd gotten the water from the bathroom instead of the kitchen. He ordered me to dump it out and go fill her cup from the kitchen sink downstairs. I said, "But the sink up here is the same as the water downstairs."

He turned to our baby daughter and said, "You tell your mommy that you are *not* gonna drink that and that she needs to go downstairs and get you water from the kitchen!"

So she obliged her daddy's order, told me to get her new water, and I obeyed. I went back to bed because it was easier to let it go and to get back to sleep rather than taking a stand at that point. But the next day I realized he was systematically teaching our daughter that the role of a mother and wife was total subservience. And I did not want her to think that was where she was guaranteed to end up as a grown woman. So my first motivation to face the pain of change was simply a desire to set a healthier example for my daughter.

My second motivation came when my physical health broke down so badly that without the intervention of modern medicine I probably would not be alive today. As a result of the intense stress in our home, I had a strong anaphylactic reaction on an ongoing basis. My body broke out in hives that were only barely controllable with steroid treatments. It was so bad that the steroids were the only thing keeping my airways open enough to breathe. It controlled the hives so they were only itchy, swollen, and painful, but not life-threatening. My doctors determined that I actually had no allergies and my anaphylaxis and hives were being triggered by chronic stress.

A full year later, the hives were still only barely under control, and I finally accepted that this destructive dichotomy between internal and external values in our home had to be dealt with for my own personal survival. Agonizingly, I decided to start a new life on my own. It has been an ongoing journey as far as giving my daughter an example of an emotionally healthy woman in the context of life, marriage, and parenting. My health dramatically improved almost overnight.

Faced with choices where it seemed like there was no good option, Holly chose to focus on re-establishing her equilibrium after living for years in the toxic shadow of someone else's double life. In the end, the only way to achieve a life lived with one face for herself, was to strike out on her own.

NO MAN (OR WOMAN) IS AN ISLAND

Every person would prefer to assume that our personal choices affect no one but ourselves. It's easier to excuse and rationalize inconsistency that way. But that simply isn't reality. If you choose not to live according to one authentic set of values, you are ultimately forcing the people around you into unthinkable sets of choices they would not otherwise face. This applies in marital relationships, business relationships, friendships, and anywhere we interact with other people.

Holly continues:

> My top five values are *faith*, *hope*, *love*, *integrity*, and *loyalty*. When you value loyalty and you choose to extend that loyalty to someone, you risk that they may not have the same value. If that other person doesn't live with integrity, or as you say, with one face, it becomes very difficult to choose between your other values and the value of loyalty. And it puts you in a difficult situation.

There is no such thing as a neutral choice. Holly's experience is a painful illustration of how choices may be moral, immoral, or amoral, but never neutral. The person you are and the person you will become, is constantly being molded by the decisions you make, no matter how small. Your identity is always moving in one direction or another.

Every choice is a fork in the road. By default, when you do not choose the other fork, you're becoming a certain type of person. Every choice contributes in its own small way to shaping your identity, strengthening or weakening your character, becoming more aligned with or diverting you away from your core values.

Holly's journey continued after striking out on her own as a single mother. Her hives completely disappeared shortly after she moved out, and they never came back. She processed by writing a lot in the first years after she left. One of her diary entries chronicles the realization that she was now free to eat Life cereal, which her ex-husband had forbidden from the house. She could even have a second bowl or eat it all day if she wanted. It sounds like such a small thing, but when someone forbids you from eating something or bringing it into the house, that freedom becomes a big deal. Yes, it's just cereal. But it was one of the things that figured largely into her experience of learning to re-own her identity. She began to take back who she was as a person. Something as apparently neutral as cereal was an indicator of how much of herself she had given over to outside control.

It was not a neutral choice. Life cereal, to Holly, represented regaining the independence of her identity.

"In a healthy relationship, it shouldn't matter whether or not you eat Life cereal," Holly continues. "What matters is whether the values underpinning any decision are rooted in a commitment to the integrity of the relationship. If so, you're making that choice for a reason, which means it's definitely not a neutral choice because the purpose is the good of the relationship."

MEASURE YOUR INTENTIONS

If no choice is neutral, then every single thing you do requires a sense of consciousness about the intention behind it. That's where knowing your core values can help you stay connected to the deeper identity your actions stem from.

Your marriage may be just fine. Or maybe you're not married at all. Regardless, there are lessons to be gleaned from Holly's experience that hold the power to transform your success in any other collaborative relationship. If you have drifted from your internal values compass—either as a result of your own choices or due to being swept into the choices made by someone else—perhaps it's time to reconsider your own set of values and think about initiating a turnaround.

If you've already completed the Values Discovery exercise from Chapter 3, and you know you've drifted off course from those values, then you may already be pondering ways to reestablish your identity, recapture ownership of who you really are, and realign yourself with your core values.

LIVING IN A POWER IMBALANCE

Have you submitted to someone else's value system (or lack thereof), hoping to keep the peace? As a result of a flawed expectation of submission or obedience, have you sacrificed your workplace identity and found yourself going along with things that you don't feel comfortable with? Or are you the one wielding all the power and bending others to your will?

An imbalance of power can make someone feel that, in order to stay in the good graces of the person who holds greater power, they must deny or ignore aspects of their identity, preferences, or value system. Then, you're introducing an unhealthy and potentially destructive situation. You're forcing at least one person in the equation to live a face that is lying and ultimately denying them freedom to follow the values that are authentic to their identity. Power imbalance often results when leaders in the position of higher power lack the personal insight to recognize when someone's conflict-resolution style is accommodating or compromising. In effect, the other person is going along because they are just trying to reduce conflict. In Holly's situation, the conflict arose because she wanted to have a value system that never shifted regardless of environment or onlookers.

Holly says:

I wanted our values to be consistently the same when we were out and about, or at church, or socializing, or at work and anywhere else. I wanted our values to be the same in our home as well. But my way of dealing with conflict was to be as accommodating as possible. As a result, I let go of a lot of things that were actually meaningful to me. I've seen that happen in my work experience as well, when a decision was handed down that I had to carry out, but I just felt sick doing so.

I realized that I needed to ask myself some incredibly difficult questions. How do I change the way I carry out my values so that there is cohesion between my workplace, my social life, and my family life? How do I make certain that my values are clearly known and carried out on my part and that everyone else knows where I stand?

Holly's choice to regain a values-driven identity was the beginning of her journey back into living with one face.

TURNAROUND IS POSSIBLE

As I've been working on this book, people have often asked what I'm writing about. When I tell them, some respond that they feel sometimes people get so far down the road of living with multiple faces that there's no turning back. They say that they know someone who really wants to be a moral person, but who started out taking small steps toward cutthroat business decisions, or abusive power management, or accommodating conflict instead of standing up to it. Then, that aspect that denies their core values, whatever it is, eventually becomes an integrated part of their identity. And they start to lose hope.

I can't help but wonder when people tell me this, if they are using the stories of vague and unnamed friends to cover their own sense of hopelessness. I wonder if they've gotten to a point where having the desire to change is not enough, because they feel completely overwhelmed by how far apart their internal and external sets of values have drifted from each other.

Is it possible for someone who has been led down the path of living with multiple faces to turn around? Is it possible to transform back to the place where the person they see in the mirror is someone they actually respect? Where their identity consists of only one face?

I asked Holly those exact questions.
She replied:

Absolutely. I believe it is possible.

But is it easy? Absolutely not. Embracing the path of *living with one face*, when you've lost your way, invites all sorts of criticism from the outside. We like to celebrate the stories of people who did an about-face in life, unless we kind of knew them already. The shallow observers in your life may be completely incapable of understanding why you're making this choice to change. They may even view your intentional steps toward change as evidence that you are adrift, because it's very different than your previous choices.

The thing to remember is that it's totally okay if outsiders don't get it, because they aren't the ones who have to look in your mirror every morning and respect the person you see looking back at you. I mean, hey, I lived an entire year with full body hives before I finally took the step to embrace radical change in my life and bring my values and my reality back into alignment with each other. Executing a successful, values-driven turnaround is going to be difficult, but it is not impossible.

THREE KEYS TO SUCCESSFUL TURNAROUND

If you want to get back to your original value system, there are a few key strategies that will help you find success. First, of course, you need to reassess what those core values actually are for you, and you need to give some thought to which secondary values stem from those core values.

For example, the value of loyalty does not stand alone. Loyalty actually stems from the core value of love. It takes a journey down into your soul to figure out, "This is who I actually am, and this is how that identity plays out in my life." You won't know the answers right away, but they will come.

1. **Take your time and allow for mistakes.** Give yourself a chance to mentally and emotionally explore how you ended up where you are. Process the journey of little choices that got you here. Assess your daily interactions with people to discover where you're continuing to make choices that are out of alignment with the person you want to be. You're not going to jump back into perfect alignment with your values without making some missteps. The point is to learn from them, not to succumb to them.

2. **Reject habitual reactions.** Step back from choices that seem easy. Consider whether you're making this decision based on a misaligned comfort zone, or if it is truly the wisest choice. Take some space to breathe and find a new footing in your personal and spiritual relationships. And avoid knee-jerk reactions that are likely to stem from the values system that you want to shed.

3. **Implement a solid decision-making framework.** Go back to Chapter 4 and reread the section on willpower

and your four advisors. Put every new choice through those four questions, without fail. And if you have weak willpower, find an accountability partner who will keep you on track to follow through with whatever decisions your four advisors reveal to be correct.

Depending on how far you've drifted out of alignment, you may actually have to relearn how to live out the core values that you cherish. It will take time and commitment to re-establish a one-faced identity. You may find that the stakes rise as you become more and more aligned, and people's expectations of you grow higher, because they instinctively feel they can now trust you more fully. That also means that if and when you screw up, it's going to be that much more painful. But it isn't any less crucial.

Choosing change over comfort can be excruciating. But when you know that you are the active ingredient in your decisions—these choices are neither foisted upon you nor passively accepted by you—then you can find freedom in the reality that making mistakes is no longer the same as living with multiple faces.

When you choose change, you are not catapulting toward perfection. Instead, you are committing to take responsibility for your choices and to embrace a path that leads toward alignment with your core values, regardless of the consequences. Daring greatly may mean making decisions that are proven to be mistakes but were driven by a desire to live true to your values. It also means that when you mess up, you're responsible enough to make it right at any cost.

The primary questions that you must answer for yourself are these:

1. Do you cherish your integrity more than *anything* else?
2. Are your values more valuable to you than any other perk or consequence?

CHAPTER 9

MENTOR POWER

Try not to become a man of success. Rather become a man of value.

—Albert Einstein

Ever since my mother found me curled up in a corner with a pencil and a notebook crafting stories for imaginary characters around age 7, I've been a writer and storyteller. But I've realized that the underlying platform in my career has not been focused on *how* to tell a story, because it doesn't matter what stories you're telling if your internal and external values are not driven by the same platform, the same level of integrity.

This book actually started out as a guide on how to tell stories beautifully. A few thousand words into it, I realized storytelling isn't the main point, so I scrapped most of that content and started over. Maybe someday I'll write that book for its own sake (yes, of course I kept the files, I'm a nerd, remember?), but the foundation underpinning any story is the understanding of how to live in harmony with one's values. Every great story flows out of the challenge of making great choices—and the battle between whether you'll go against your conscience or embrace the more difficult path of honor.

DO IT BETTER

Many business owners feel compelled to provide something completely unique and original in order to find success. But that's not necessarily the key to success. Filling a niche and rising to the top can also be achieved by stepping into a space that is already overwhelmed with options, but where all those options have something lacking. If you step into a niche and you do it with clearly defined values—better systems than everybody else, with higher quality, kinder service, stronger team loyalty, and better overall brand story—people will pay more because they crave the chance to trust that someone out there is both who and what they say they are. That can be you.

One key component among the most successful brands, be they people or industry leading corporate organizations, is a sense of predictability that translates into trust. Instead of capitalizing on a quick-fix, they fixate on long-term impact, which ultimately translates into predictability. When your organization is predictable, that means people instinctively trust you, because you said so.

Cory Bergeron is a rock star in the TV sales world, author of Thousands Per Minute, and owner of the Tampa-based video sales company Pitch Video. During his stint on the Home Shopping Network, he sold more than $100,000,000 worth of products. Not because he's the slickest salesman, but because he understands the importance of building trust. He's the kind of guy people know they can count on. With Cory, what you see is what you get, and everybody knows it. If Cory says this product will perform a certain way in your home, then you can trust that, because Cory said it, that's exactly what will exactly happen. He's known for being straightforward, honest, and trustworthy.

When I asked him how he had achieved that long-lasting career quality and being known so well for living with one face, he credited two sources: his upbringing and his mentors.

He says:

My mother is an amazing woman, I didn't even believe she was human until about 2006. My step-father came into my life when I was 6 and raised me until I left home at 18. He was a bricklayer and a pastor, a very hard-working man. After he passed away, I got to read his journals and discovered that he didn't enjoy bricklaying just for the creativity. He actually enjoyed bricklaying because he got to be around other tough men. He loved that environment of hard-working guys who told it like it was, who didn't mince words, who weren't afraid to break their backs every day and go home knowing they earned their dinner. From him, I got a strong love of the outdoors, a respect for literature, an appreciation for critical thinking. He was fiercely committed to his family, extremely hard-working, and immovable when it came to his morals.

I think a lot of that had to do with the man I have grown into. You could almost consider me a little obsessive compulsive about my values. Because of my fiercely loyal nature to my family, friends, and responsibilities, I tend to shy away from places where I feel my integrity would be questioned. It's a challenge doing what I do for a living because lots of people go on the air and sell products on television who are more than willing to tell you the whatever hogwash is necessary to get you to pick up the phone and dial so they can make the sale.

Me, on the other hand, I'm more concerned with the long-term payoff. I'm more concerned about telling you exactly what you can expect. And about you being able to replicate those exact results, in your own home, with the product I am going to send you. I want to have you come back afterwards and say, "I absolutely love this thing!" I'd love to hear that.

The political climate of any kind of television network can be absolutely cutthroat. It's an environment where you either cut throats or your own throat will get cut. Consequently, many people who try to have a morally sound business life have watched as their integrity failed them. They'll do just about anything to keep a job and feed their families, so they feel they have to change their values and do whatever is necessary to survive. I know some feel that they could never rewrite their script. It would almost require an entire industry change for them to be free to make that happen in the TV network world.

Many who have gone far enough down that unethical path are seen as fierce, do-whatever-it-takes individuals. They are high-ranking powerful people, but if they lost their powerful jobs, I'm not sure that they could go somewhere else in this industry. They had to be cutthroat to get there, and now they have to be cutthroat to stay. And they can't easily leave and start fresh elsewhere, because they've established a ruthless reputation that will tarnish any new role. I don't want to focus on the negative, but there are people who definitely face this dilemma.

I didn't start out as a TV product salesman. I was a lowly crew manager first. And the man who was my boss showed me what it meant to do right no matter what. John was a powerful leader, full of integrity to the point of fault. His personal values were so strong that he eventually risked his livelihood and family to stay true to them.

As a younger team leader, it was nice to know that somebody with that kind of integrity had my back. It empowered me to do the right thing even in touchy situations. Knowing that if I was at fault (and many times I was), I could step up and say "I'm really sorry about this. This is totally on my shoulders. I'm not gonna put it on anyone else. This is what I'm gonna do to make sure that this won't happen again." It also gave me freedom to confront team members, before they raise their finger and say, "I have an issue with you."

Before John came, the atmosphere at work was despondent. People came to work every day hating their jobs, lining up at the time clock to wait that last extra minute so they can punch back out and escape. Everyone was underpaid. Even the desk chairs were falling apart. Nobody was doing anything about it. Simple comforts make a big difference in morale, but it wasn't taken care of. Everyone pointed fingers at each other's departments saying, "You guys aren't doing this. You guys aren't doing that."

Then John arrived. He called a meeting of all 180 production staff and said, "As of this moment, we stop pointing the finger at any other department. No one here is allowed to speak up and tell anybody else that they have failed to do their job, or they haven't done something right. We are gonna take everybody else's crap that they have not done properly, we are gonna be the last line of defense, and we are gonna do everybody else's job better than they have done it. And we are gonna do it willingly, knowing that it's not our job, knowing that it's another department's job and they've been failing the whole time. And when we have done that for an entire year, you will have empowered me to sit down at a meeting and start yanking out everybody else's skeletons. They will not be able to point their finger at us, because we will be the shining example of what this company needs to be. They will not be able to find a single fault with us. And then I will be in a position to start discussing wages for the people who deserve it, and proper chairs so your backs aren't hurting all day, and better bathroom facilities. We are going to step up and be the bigger people here, instead of just sitting at the table and doing the name-calling at everybody else."

John inspired our entire department to become character-driven. And it changed everything. After that year of hard work and zero complaining, he went to human resources and said, "We have people who've been with our company for 20 years and do better work than anybody else in the industry. They're getting paid less than newbies right out of high school. This needs to change right now. And here's the rest of what needs to be fixed..." They said, "We'll take care of it."

Next he went to the merchandising department and then the producers and so on, and each time he said, "We've been doing your job for a long time. But it's supposed to be your job. We need you to step up, or we need you to step down."

And because of the integrity and change he had developed in his own department, the people higher up said, "This is wonderful. Please advise other departments how to do what you did."

By the end of that year, they got new chairs and people got paid more. But morale actually improved even before the rewards kicked in because there was open communication. Everybody in the department knew what we were aiming for and what the end game was. They also knew nobody had done it before. One huge morale booster was the boss himself. So many decisions had traditionally been made by administrators who never entered the studio, guys who sat behind a desk and made calls out of total ignorance. John would skip work all day on Wednesdays to come in at 7 p.m. and pull the overnight shift with the crew—to be with them in the middle of the night and hear what they had to say on the front line. Everybody knew he had two boys and a wife. He wasn't some single guy that could easily do this. He was taking time away from his family, destroying his sleep schedule, doing whatever necessary to make sure he was in the trenches with his team on a regular basis, hearing direct feedback and getting involved.

More than once, a crew member got sick and had to go home, leaving us short staffed on set. So John, a Vice President, would take off his tie, throw on a team shirt, and go out on the floor to pull cameras. Nobody does that! The supervisors wouldn't even do that. And here's this guy three levels above them coming down and digging his hands in. The crew respected him so much.

Middle management loved him. Because of him, they could live with integrity; they could do what they felt was right. And even if things went to hell in hand-basket, they knew he had their back. He would face anyone in top management and say, "I am standing in solidarity with this low person on the totem pole to tell you that they were right in doing this." And that was powerful.

John's concern was looking himself square in the eye in the mirror every night and knowing that he respected the guy looking back. He was determined to do an absolute 200% knock-up job on anything that he sunk his mind into.

I asked Cory, "How would you describe the core values that drive your public and private life and do you even know what they would be if you had to name them?" He chuckled with the confidence of someone completely at peace with himself, as though it was ludicrous that anyone might *not* know the principles that defined their daily existence.

He replied:

Authenticity. Being concerned first and foremost with the welfare of my clients rather than the success of my business.

Other-centeredness—I have many opportunities to sell people a whole lot more than what I sold them, but instead I focus on selling what is right for them at that time and make sure they don't overspend.

Under-promise and over-deliver—do more than people expect. For my video clients, I lay out exactly what their video is gonna look like, but I always look for an opportunity to shoot that extra scene or do that little effect that will blow their mind and I put it in the video without telling them.

Transparency—you can't be transparent without being authentic, but they aren't the same thing. Authenticity is a lifestyle whereas transparency is more associated with having open communication.

WHAT TO DO—WHAT NOT TO DO

Some mentors will keep you on track because they are so incredibly authentic and committed. Others are so crazy they probably ought to *be* committed. You can learn from both— sometimes recognizing what you should do, other times acknowledging that the lesson lies firmly in how not to lead.

The boss in my opening story gifted me with lifelong leadership lessons in how not to lead a team. His lack of respect fostered deep distrust and a constant sense of self-preservation among the team. During the years I worked for him, as I managed our international team, I realized that most of them would do anything for me because I always had their back, and if I messed up, I'd honestly tell them I had.

On the other hand, my boss's operating philosophy was more along the lines of "expect humanly impossible accomplishments, and throw the team under the bus when mistakes are made." Whenever we did a great job, he would take all the credit and rarely mention that he even had a support team.

MENTOR POWER

Your best mentors might be the ones who model exactly what to do. Or, like too many of mine, they might give you a front row seat to what poor management looks like. You can learn invaluable lessons either way, if you're willing to absorb them.

Rejecting the mentors available to you can result in frustration and failure, sometimes at great cost. If you're aiming for greatness in personal morality and business achievement, don't overlook the power of solid mentorship.

CONVERSATIONS | NED LOTT | DISNEY AND PIXAR

If there's any industry that knows something about creating an engaging, multi-sensory, story-driven brand experience, it's Hollywood. Thanks to some work I've done with an independent feature film, a friend introduced me to Ned Lott, a producer and voice-casting director, for Oscar nominees and blockbusters from Disney, Pixar, and other studios. He's worked with huge projects such as Chronicles of Narnia, Frozen, Monsters Inc., Pirates of the Caribbean, Cars, Lord of the Rings, The Lego Movie Video Game, and more.

Sarah: What is it about the human experience that gives some films that sense of greatness, even animated films? What threads weave between movies that stand out and movies that fail? When a movie falls short of greatness because X is lacking, what do you believe is X? And how can business leaders learn from it?

Ned: This is a great question. There's actually been a significant shift. Movie success used to be defined as films full of originality, but these days the ones making money aren't original at all. They're all extensions in series like Marvel, set in familiar contexts rather than movies like the Matrix, which were highly original but completely unfamiliar. But the current trend is that nobody wants to view originality.

The last Oscars were filled with nominations for independent movies that nobody watched. If you look at their box office levels, it's hilarious because they hardly made any money. The ones that made money are the sequels, the comic book heroes, the fantasy sequels. And then there was the 50 Shades of Grey franchise, which caused a huge stir around the world because of the morality of it all.

Sarah: Right. Or perhaps the absence of morality of it all.

Ned: Exactly! Why was that so successful? Because it's like the Twilight franchise. It was a big novel, and they didn't even have to make the movie very good. Just as long as it's based on that novel, you have an audience. It's really nothing original.

Sarah: What about the films that are marketed as Bible or faith based? Have those been more driven by values, in your opinion?

Ned: When the big films Exodus and Noah came out, they were just so weird. I had to see them; I wanted to know what's going on. But it was just bizarre.

When we were developing the first Chronicles of Narnia film, we were so careful to make sure it was accurate. We had pastors on board, and the C.S. Lewis Estate, to ensure accuracy to the original material and authenticity to our target audience's expectations. With The Passion of the Christ, it was exact same thing. And the Christian community embraced both movies.

Sarah: Right.

Ned: Interestingly, during the second Narnia movie, the director of the movie decided to move a different direction and basically said, "Ok, thanks guys for your help. We're going to do this one on our own." They ignored the pastors, they ignored the C.S. Lewis Estate, and as a result, the Prince Caspian film is not that close to the book. And the result? It was a disappointment at the box office.

We tried to tell these guys, "There is a reason why the first one was so big. Because we were honoring the material it came from. Because we were respecting the pastors and historians!"

After the second Narnia film was such a disappointment, they came back to us and said, "Ok, let's go back to the novel's original material. Back to the pastors for guidance."

But then the Noah and Exodus films approached the narratives as an opportunity to completely create a new story.

Sarah: So you're saying that one of the reasons Narnia and Passion were such huge hits was because they stayed true and authentic to the original material. They honored the values that had built the stories in the first place.

Ned: Yes! They honored the values, and they honored their audience. They went to the experts and said, "How can we stay true to the material?" Those values gave the final product a sense of authenticity and respect that won over loyal audiences. With the Passion, they went before Billy Graham; they went before the Pope. They went to all these leaders and said, "We need your approval," and that's what we also did with the first Narnia film. When movie-makers get arrogant and say, "We don't need to honor the original material," it never turns out well. When they get focused on the bottom line, the box office, the potential DVD sales, and ignore the audience, they're not going to support you.

Sarah: You're going to lose your target audience.

Ned: And they completely lost the audience. Then some ask, "Why would we do a Biblical movie?" But there's still a bunch of them in the works. So you hope somebody, sometime, gets it right. Soon.

Sarah: This is a huge take-away for business leaders! The common thread that runs between the really successful films is that: 1) they know where they are coming from, 2) they honor who they are and the story they're telling, and 3) they honor a deep and well-researched understanding of the audience that is going to buy from them.

If they are not true to the content of the story, the values of the story, and the primary audience for the story, then it is highly likely to fall short at the box office.

Ned: Yes, exactly. Value and integrity is key for productions, but it goes for every other line of business as well. Know your audience, and you'll hit gold. That's what we learned at Disney. With the different characters, we always would say, "You've got to keep the integrity to how they were created. Whether it's a good message or a bad message, you have to show that, so whenever you see them, you know what they're going to do."

Sarah: Right, so in other words, you need to know your characters so well that there's a predictability. You also need to know your audience so well that you know what will make them excited and responsive.

Ned: You can't destroy your audience; you have to maintain their reputation. You know when people meet celebrities and get disappointed by them? You can't let that happen with your characters. You can't let your target audience feel that the characters have let them down.

Sarah: Same thing in business. If you put out a certain image in your marketing, before someone comes to your place of business or experiences your products or service, and you say: "We stand for this particular worldview. We're all about integrity; we're all about values. Then they come, and if it's not like that, they feel like they've been given a bait and switch. If your client has a different experience than you advertised, or the experience doesn't translate to them as being consistent with what you said you stand for, then you didn't just lose a customer—you may have gained an antagonist.

I would venture to say that in personal leadership, it is also very much the same. If someone presents themselves as being an honest, trustworthy person, but you find out they are not living with one face, it hurts. When you discover that some great guy at work is actually beating his wife at home, there is this sense of betrayal, and it runs very deep.

Ned: Just look at The Cosby Show and how that was tarnished. He's been basically burned at the stake, and as a result, his brand is destroyed forever. It will never be the same. How sad that is...

Sarah: And the terrible part is that whether or not Cosby was living his brand in private, he had a lot of good things to say, that a lot of people needed to hear. But because his personal reputation has taken such a hit, everything good that he had to say is now suspect. You must stay true to what you say that you stand for. People want to be free to respect those who they believe are worthy of it.

For people who are living multiple faces and switching between values, it is an incredible amount of stress to maintain multiple sets of values and be a different type of person, depending on which venue or environment you're in. It's no wonder people get sick from the stress. If one (or more!) of your faces is lying, that is constant stress, because you must always keep track of what you say and who you are to different people.

Ned: Yes.

Sarah: There's an incredible amount of peace in being governed by the same values all the time. Whether you're in film or in business or a non-profit or something else, when you screw up (and we ALL screw up), when you make those mistakes, you have to own them. You have to be brave enough to say, "Hey, I messed up. That is not the kind of person I'm trying to be. I'm really sorry. And now I'm going to go back and keep on trying to be the kind of person I want to be." Instead of hiding it.

Ned: In my career, especially with freelance, people see the projects I'm attached to, and they bring me on board because they know I'm going to take good care of their film's characters. There is going to be integrity in it, and I will not allow those characters to wander off into some moral abyss.

Sarah: Low ground.

Ned: There's trust based not only on the projects I've completed, but also because of the projects I've turned down. Sometimes I'll get a feeler for a project that isn't a good fit for my values, and I don't even have to say "No" because it just disappears. It's like panning for gold; the muck and mire disappears, but the gold stays on top. Because I've chosen to stay true to the values that drive my brand, my reputation, and my work.

Sarah: I often hear business owners say something like, "A lot of people would like to do business that way, but it's just really not possible. You can't make money on the up and up. It's impossible to live without skeletons in your closet. You simply can't be honest and make money or be successful." What would you say to someone who thinks that they cannot have integrity without losing business?

Ned: I just can't imagine having to go through life like that. In the '90s, I worked with The Learning Company; we were the leading group on educational software then. Remember Reader Rabbit and Where in the World is Carmen San Diego? We got bought out, and the new owners wanted our whole team to stay. Our entire group shared these values unitedly. One day, the new owners came in and said, "We want you guys to produce the Sports Illustrated Swimsuit calendar CD-ROM."

My boss called us into a room and said, "OK guys, we have a chance to make a lot of money with this, but I want to get all your input, because this isn't what we signed up to do here. We've always had values that don't include selling sex. We almost unanimously agreed it wasn't appropriate. It wasn't appropriate for us because of the values we held as a team, but also from a business standpoint. A sexy product was incompatible with the audience we had chosen to build.

Sarah: In other words, it would not be consistent with the brand you had built for your team.

Ned: Right! If you're facing a values conflict, and you're not the boss, you can't always go to your CEO and say, "I think this is offensive." Your boss will just say, "No problem, we'll give the jobs to someone else." But you can approach your leadership and share how something may be off-brand for your audience. "This is not good for your bottom line. You're going to alienate your audience and lose their trust." We told our CEO this when we declined the swimsuit project, and he ended up refusing to sign the contract.

Sarah: That's genius. Instead of making it personal if you have a values conflict at work, focus on the expectations of your audience. If they have grown to expect a certain level of morality, of trustworthiness, then unethical actions or a breakdown in values would be crossing that boundary and giving your audience that feeling of betrayal.

Ned: An unethical shortcut is never worth risking alienation from your audience! I just can't imagine living that way.

Sarah: No matter where you are on the trajectory of building a business, if you are dedicated to loyalty toward your core values, there may be attrition before there is growth. But once you are known for being trustworthy, the growth will be far greater than the attrition.

Ned: Nothing's guaranteed success, but at least your life will be successful. And it might open door to something else. I see some entrepreneurs ruining their reputations with all the little shortcuts. They always want pay under the table, or they don't pay their taxes. But I don't know of anyone like that who's become super successful. They're often miserable. And secretive. Always asking for discounts, always scrimping like misers. Show me a person who has been super successful when they do that behind the scenes.

Sarah: Can't think of any!

Ned: Living contrary to your values is like being in prison. Living loyal to your values is a release from those handcuffs because your ethics say you don't do any of those duplicitous things in the first place.

Hiding nothing means you are free to put all your energy into positive activities and building your business. It's total freedom.

CHAPTER 10

GO FORWARD | THINK BACKWARD

[The race is] not to the strong, it's to those who hold on...
It's not to the swift, it's to those who persist.
—Nwamiko Madden

S o how can you build a sustainable corporate brand or personal reputation that stands the test of time? And how can you cultivate a culture around yourself that lends toward the mentorship of other leaders who are prepared to step into key roles and maintain the values standards you've set for your company?

I sat down with Andrew Benton, president of Pepperdine University, to ask these same questions. Andrew has cultivated a long-standing legacy of leadership at one of the premier private universities in the United States and has the unique advantage of also seeing many of his graduates go on to become phenomenally successful individuals of integrity.

Pepperdine's core values are two-fold:

1. to be successful, we must be deeply Christian, and
2. to compete well in the world, we must be academically strong.

If you ask Andrew Benton, the secret sauce at Pepperdine is their quest to be both good and true at the same time. In other words, their values are excellence and authenticity. And their mantra is that to fail at one is to fail. The two core values are a package, and their success is either achieved by both or nothing.

So, how has Pepperdine managed to build a sustainable, values-driven corporate culture that stands the test of time? "Two things," Andrew says.

First, mission matters most. We want to be academically outstanding, we want our faculty publishing, we want to keep the best and brightest students, but we can never lose sight of the mission. It's discouraging sometimes, but one of my favorite phrases is, "We refuse to choose." We refuse to choose between academic excellence and faith-based values. It's a false argument to say that you've got to choose; you do not. You can do both. You *must* do both.

THREE WAYS TO SUCCEED IN VALUES-DRIVEN BUSINESS

I asked Andrew, "If you were to speak to younger entrepreneurs or leaders and distill your best, most practical advice to guide their launch into values-driven leadership and business, what would you say?"

He replied:

First of all, *create alignment in your life*. Don't work for a company that doesn't square with who you are, or who want to be, because you'll always be unhappy.

Second, if you can find an organization where you can thrive and enjoy a complete merger of your personal life and your professional life, then *render yourself invaluable* within the organization, and you will always have a great job.

Third, *be a truth teller*, be an individual who inspires confidence. Because when you find that perfect alignment of your personal self and your professional self, it's a gift that can last a lifetime.

I absolutely believe it is possible to maintain integrity, live authentic to your values, and be wildly successful in business. I see it happening all the time. Not just in my own sphere of higher education, but I know some very fine lawyers, architects, and medical doctors who wear the exact same face all day in all situations, and I honor them.

It's a decision you must make pretty early in life—that that's just simply how it's gonna be for you. I also know plenty of people who have stumbled because they stopped thinking about those things that are underlying yet so important, so fundamental.

But those who have lived with that consistency, with one face as you say, and those who are living with one face right now, I believe they will be successful for the rest of their career.

ALONE WE DRIFT

At whatever point you were in your leadership experience when you opened the first page of this book, I hope you're not still stuck in the same spot. If I'm honest, I'm hoping you've moved down the path of continued authentic growth or transparent turnaround. Either way, I also hope you're not trying to do it all alone.

Douglas Copeland, author of *Applied Microeconomics*, says, "Inspiration is both a tool and a trap. If you're going to be inspired by anyone, be inspired by people who have been exactly where you are now." This brings us to the question: How can I actively embrace the wisdom of mentors and colleagues to help myself and my business stay on brand and maintain authenticity to my articulated values?

Alone, we drift. In order to move forward powerfully, you need to surround yourself with mentors and peers who hold you accountable to authentic values and keep you focused on what matters most.

Whether you are a leader in your workplace, a public figure, or at the helm of a company aspiring to become a leading brand among your competitors, it doesn't matter. Whether you run a massive international operation or a small business, the need for congruency between internal and external applies equally. You may have a public life and a private life as a company, a small business, or as a celebrity. But those two environments absolutely must be governed by the same set of values.

As you close this book and go forward, I want you to also think backward. Ponder what has gotten you here and how you can adjust in order to live according to your values. This book is full of stories proving it can be done. The question is, will your life prove the same?

Are you ready to change? Here's what you need to say:

"I don't like the two or 10 or 1,000 different identities staring me back in the mirror. I want to choose one person to be. I'm going to get rid of all this extra stress in my life that results from living a fractured identity that is not true to my core values. I'm ready to acknowledge that, as a result, there's likely to be a lot of attrition in my life. I'm probably going to lose some of the things that have made me comfortable, but it's going to be worth it in the end."

Because you know what? It is *absolutely* going to be worth it in the end.

ABOUT THE AUTHOR

Sarah McDugal is a director, producer, strategist, and leadership speaker. She creates Hollywood-quality brand campaigns for companies who value their impact on people as much as on their bottom line.

Sarah's media career launched as the teenaged host of an international Christian TV show. Since then, she has produced and directed more than 150 short films and TV shows, from city-wide message campaigns to national franchise branding to global satellite TV network programs. She has managed production teams internationally as creative director, producer, and talent coach. In 2014, she directed a music video officially nominated for Video of the Year at the Canadian Gospel Music Awards.

In 2012, Sarah launched her own branding company, creating compelling messages in the USA and abroad for national medical franchises, non-profit hospital systems, educational organizations, humanitarian aid foundations, and more.

A dedicated mother, lover of international vegetarian cuisine, avid reader and global traveler, Sarah has visited or worked in more than 40 countries but remains convinced that her passport feels neglected.

Printed in the USA
CPSIA information can be obtained
at www.ICGtesting.com
JSHW082349140824
68134JS00020B/1981

9 781630 477325